The Reel Classroom

AN INTRODUCTION TO FILM STUDIES AND FILMMAKING

The Reel Classroom

JEFF DANIELIAN & URIAH DONNELLY

ILLUSTRATED BY WILLIAM SCHAFF

PRUFROCK PRESS INC.
WACO, TEXAS

DEDICATION

For Mike, the dog. –Jeff

For Elwood. –Uriah

ACKNOWLEDGMENTS

Jeff would like to thank:

Bro. Phillip Bergeron, the first teacher of film studies I ever had, who opened my eyes to the world of cinematic history. Professor Art Numora at Loyola Marymount University, who not only provided me with the tools and skills I needed, but also supported my ideas and visions. Elissa Cerros, whose guidance and assistance over the years have gone above and beyond my expectations. Vittorio De Sica, for *The Bicycle Thief*, and Chris Marker, for *La Jetée*. Uriah Donnelly, for the initial conversation that led to this work, the understanding of what it means to coauthor a book, and his friendship. My daughter, Grace, for her creativity and spontaneity—it rubs off on me. My son, Cooper, for lightsaber battles and walks down the road. My wife, Samantha, for putting up with yet another season of writing.

Uriah would like to thank:

Dr. Michael Skeldon, for mentoring me through my time at Beacon and for teaching me how to teach. Dr. Bonnie MacDonald; I wouldn't be where I am today if not for her staunch support of me as a film educator and as a person. Dr. Claudia Springer, for helping me find my path after a rocky start to my college career and unconditional guidance along the way. Jeff Danielian, for his knowledge of and commitment to education; it is inspiring. Without him, this book would be just jumbled thoughts on a page. My father, Elwood, for introducing me to the beautiful world of cinema; you are my role model and support system. My wife, Janet, for allowing me to love you. "The greatest thing you'll ever learn, is just to love and be loved in return."

Uriah and Jeff would like to thank:

It was a pleasure working with our editor, Rachel Taliaferro, whose love of film is in sync with ours. Our manuscript reviewers, for their careful review of the initial drafts of this text. The folks at Café Zog, Tea in Sahara, and Kris Hansen's Speakeasy, for providing the space in which to create. William Schaff, for his inspiring illustrations. Lastly, thanks to all of the students who have sat before us throughout the years. This one is for you.

Prufrock Press Inc.
P.O. Box 8813
Waco, TX 76714-8813
Phone: (800) 998-2208
Fax: (800) 240-0333
http://www.prufrock.com

TABLE OF CONTENTS

PREFACE

My first exposure to the medium of film didn't come until I was a sophomore in high school. Of course, just like everyone else my age, I was an avid viewer of movies. I had my favorites. For me, it was all about the story. I loved the way characters seem to jump off the screen and invade my thoughts. Plots had my mind spinning. Special effects were cool. I knew little about how films were made and never appreciated the time, energy, and thought that went into them.

That was until I sat in my first film class. I was bombarded with *La Jetée, Bicycle Thieves, Double Indemnity,* and *Citizen Kane.* Chaplin and Keaton ruled the comedic stage. Leni Riefenstahl's *Triumph of the Will* blew me away. Each and every class brought with it something new to learn. I began to see past the story. I watched films frame by frame, the way they were intended to be watched. The work of Spielberg, Coppola, Hitchcock, and Scorsese had new meaning for me. Watching a movie was never the same again.

After a short-lived career as a struggling but working film student, I moved on to science and education, but the medium and the appreciation I found have never been far from my thoughts. I reference films in class, offer afterschool activities relating to film studies, teach students how to shoot, edit, and create, all the while sharing the different aspects of filmmaking involved. I have even used film as a method of counseling known as cinematherapy.

Filmmaking is powerful, and when I think back, my only regret is that this awakening happened when today's technology didn't exist yet. Oh, and as the medium moved from film to digital, the materials have become much, much cheaper and easier to obtain. Now, more than ever, the floor is the students.'

—Jeff Danielian

As far back as I can remember, I have been drawn to cinema. This more than likely comes from my father. He was a film lover and would always record movies from the TV onto VHS tapes. Over the years he accumulated quite a collection of films. So, at an early age I was being introduced to Fellini, Hitchcock, and De Sica instead of watching cartoons. The Marx Brothers were also a big deal in my house growing up. My older brother and I would often reenact skits from their movies, especially *Horse Feathers* and *Duck Soup*. My folks are musicians, and early on they would be the band playing between films at a local art house theater. When I was old enough, they would let me stay and watch the feature while they went over to another gig. I saw *Bicycle Thieves*, *Hairspray*, *Mystery Train*, and many more. These were my formative years.

At the risk of sounding like a crotchety old man, film classes weren't common when I went to high school. In fact, we had only one computer. When I got to college, it didn't occur to me until junior year to take film classes. But once I did, that's all I wanted to do. Nowadays, there are countless film programs in middle and high schools all over the country.

Film has become tremendously accessible over the last decade. What used to be a trade and/or art for only some is now for all. Digital film and editing make it easy to learn and easy to master. I truly feel that all filmmakers must be film lovers first. Watch the masterpieces, watch the failures—watch them all!

—Uriah Donnelly

Although I greatly enjoy film, for the longest time I approached it like a Philistine. It is thanks to a few courses and books like this one that I have learned to appreciate film on a deeper, higher level. As a working visual artist, I am surprised I did not see the glory and beauty in each frame sooner. It wasn't until I saw the 1930 silent version of *All Quiet on the Western Front*—where scenes would end with the actors frozen in a vignette as the screen faded to black—that I really was blown away by the careful composition of all those involved in making a film.

It has been my pleasure to be involved in this project, and to get to recreate some of these wonderful and beautifully decided scenes that the authors have chosen to use to illustrate their points. That, and I really needed a ride to and from the airport. Thanks, Jeff!

—William Schaff

INTRODUCTION

Now that you have decided to explore the world of filmmaking with your students, how will you justify its worth to your colleagues and administrators, parents and naysayers? The study of film provides the opportunity to teach across disciplines; elicit emotional responses; and aid in the overall development of lifelong learning skills, a heightened world view, and stronger sense of self-concept. Learning filmmaking also involves learning cooperation, problem solving, and organizational skills.

Filmmaking as a medium has been around for over a century. In fact, movies are one of the most beloved art forms in the world. The wonder of cinema has captured the hearts and minds of people, young and old, since the Lumière brothers' first film, *La sortie des usines Lumière*, in the late 1890s. Its lasting presence, like many other art forms, has become part of the human fabric, offering commentary on the present while preserving its past. Films present situations, real or imagined, and introduce characters we recognize and identify with, people we loathe or aspire to become. We *want* to get into the lives of characters, see them succeed and fail, love and learn.

Movies offer adventure and intrigue, mystery and terror. There will be beasts and heroes, detectives and villains, lovers and fighters. We can dust our boots off in a one-horse town or journey to far-away exotic lands. At times, we may find ourselves alone. Sometimes, there are others along for the ride. Images come in black and white or vivid color. The soundtrack, silent or scored. The story, short or long. We look for clues, listen to voices, laugh, cry, and are silent. We learn. Films spark questions. They provide answers. They inform, direct, and provide an escape. What an audience experiences is only the finished product in filmmaking. It is what we download, insert, and play. And when the credits roll, we do it again.

But underlying every great film is a team of individuals that recognize, acquire, utilize, and refine skills in order to plan, imagine, and create together. Everything seen and heard is done for a reason. Watch the end credits to any film and you'll see hundreds of faceless names involved with the production. The nature of the medium necessitates collaboration of some kind. Even filmmakers who opt to write, direct, shoot, and edit their films must rely on others. To teach filmmaking is to teach the importance of working together. I wonder what *Citizen Kane* (Welles, 1941) would have been without Gregg Toland (cinematographer), Robert Wise (editor), and Bernard Herrmann (composer). Everyone involved lends a hand into the overall production. There are discussions, decisions, collaborations, and critiques.

Now, let us look at the big picture. To create a movie, people work months, sometimes years. To teach a student to make movies is to teach the three P's: preparation, planning, and patience. The results will come, but the process is hard work. A well-organized filmmaker is a good filmmaker. It is said that Hitchcock had a whole film mapped out in his head (and on paper) before production even began. By the time cameras started rolling, he was already thinking about his next project; to him, the film was already complete. That's how prepared he was. Can we expect our students to be like him? Probably not, but the better prepared and organized they are, the smoother many stages of the production process will be. Can high-quality films be made in unprepared chaos? Absolutely. But it sure makes it easier when everyone is organized!

Like any course of study, the earlier students are exposed to the concept of film studies, the better. That may sound obvious, but once the groundwork is laid and students are equipped with the tools to truly read film, the sooner they can become informed filmmakers. Most of the major American directors have also been students of film. Alfred Hitchcock (although British, he is considered an American filmmaker because the bulk of his success was in the U.S.) studied under other filmmakers before he made his first film. Steven Spielberg and Martin Scorsese went to film school. Rarely does someone just start making great films with little or no education. Quentin Tarantino may be an exception, but he was, in a sense, homeschooled. Even with no formal education, he learned from the best by watching.

Film is an extension of theater and visual arts and involves history, language arts, mathematics, science, and technology. The possibility for cross-curricular collaboration is endless. Connections can be made that will engage students who may not see film as something to be interested in for the art form. The accessibility of the medium makes it possible to watch films on TVs, computers, cell phones, and other devices. Now, more than ever, is the time to engage our students in the art of filmmaking, providing both the appreciation and knowledge to understand what is seen and heard, and insight into the skills necessary to produce a film of their own.

The goal of this text is to present both film studies and film production to students. Chapters begin with short introductions to a particular filmmaking concept, with recommendations for films to be used for screening. We'll provide sample activities and opportunities for assessment and conclude each chapter with reproducible handouts and assignment sheets. Along the way, there will be study guides, sample discussion questions, in-class exercises, and larger project ideas.

Think of this text as an introduction into the world of filmmaking from a student's perspective. Through each and every chapter, you will be guided through the main facets of the discipline, introduced to some classic directors and films, and offered the opportunity for students to create their own work. Nothing could be better than that. Page by page, and frame by frame, we'll learn about capturing the moment in the reel classroom.

Note about suggested films: Some of the films mentioned in this book may be controversial or inappropriate to some students and parents. All rated "R" films mentioned in the book are marked with an asterisk (*). It is crucial that teachers preview all of the materials prior to teaching the unit and determine what is appropriate for their own schools and classrooms. Teachers should always view selections before assigning them to students and be aware of what the school and/or district policy is on the use of materials that may be deemed controversial.

WARNING: A Film Studies course also has the potential to ruin your moving-going/watching experience for ever. In short, you'll never watch movies the same way. You'll probably ruin the experience for your friends and family as well, pointing out every single lighting design and prop motif until folks will no longer want to sit next to you. But that's what you'll want, anyway—to be left alone to watch films without the blue lights of cell phones or the rustling of candy wrappers to distract you.

CHAPTER 1

THINKING FILMICALLY
LEARNING HOW TO WATCH

The start of any comprehensive curriculum should include a chance for students to exhibit and discuss what they know, what they don't know, and what they wish to learn about the topic. Film literacy begins with an understanding of the language used and the principles involved, all within cultural and historical context. Educators can safely assume that the students seated before them have watched a number of movies, if only for the stories that they find exciting. It is crucial at this early stage for the students to understand and establish a division between what they recognize as personal taste and a higher level thinking process of evaluative judgment. Try starting class with a simple Q&A, like the one modeled in Figure 1.1.

Using this strategy is multipurposeful. First, it "breaks the ice" in the classroom by engaging students in conversation. In doing this, you engage each student right away. Having a dialogue with each of them allows you to get to know each other a little better. Second, it introduces one of the main concepts of the course: to understand *why* we watch movies. To understand film, we need to reflect on film's power to affect an audience.

> **Teacher:** What's your favorite movie?
>
> **Student:** The Hunger Games.
>
> **Teacher:** Why?
>
> **Student:** Huh?
>
> **Teacher:** Why is that your favorite?
>
> **Student:** Because . . . I like it.
>
> **Teacher:** Great. Do you like dystopian stories in general?
>
> **Student:** I . . . I don't know . . . I guess.
>
> **Teacher:** Ok.

FIGURE 1.1. SAMPLE Q & A.

ASKING WHY

When a student states that he or she likes something, educators need to ask, "Why?" When a student replies with, "Because it's good," he or she needs to be made aware that this type of response is not acceptable. Students need to come up with specific, evaluative reasons why "it's good." Try to start a conversation with a focus on why we like movies. Is it because they make us feel a certain way? What is it about movies that makes them feel the way they do? Is it the narrative, the music, the characters, or the conflict? Extensions of these discussions can lead to a knowledge web, or a way to organize all the things students know about the feelings they have. Is it a battle they enjoy, or space invaders? Why? A love story? Perhaps a good mystery? The list of questions can go on and on, but if done right, the chalk- or whiteboard will be full of topics and connections, words and phrases, all of which can then be added to students' newly forming vocabulary.

Most students go to the movies for entertainment, and there's certainly nothing wrong with that. As they enter the theater, the sights and sounds surround them. They are "unplugged." As they begin to question their own reasons "why," they will begin to plug in, absorbing the experience and gaining knowledge about what it means to evaluate the films they are watching.

Students should be instructed on how to *read* a film, much like they read a novel. Instead of the traditional page turning they are accustomed to, the "reading" starts to take place on the screen as they begin to scan the film, frame by frame, gathering information. As students learn to "read" along this curriculum, they also will begin to speak filmically, using proper terminology in the correct context. The goal is to develop a new kind of film watcher and, in turn, aid in the development of a better, more informed filmmaker.

After the class is settled the teacher can administer a film-themed Interest-a-Lyzer (Appendix G). The Interest-a-Lyzer is a questionnaire intended to encourage the students to reflect upon their own passions and interests and allow a teacher to learn about them in an informal manner.

A LITTLE FILM HISTORY

Movies are a social medium. Our students' lives are filled with them. They watch movies alone and together, and they connect with people who like and dislike the same films. They can be found quoting lines of dialogue, and often insert them into everyday conversations. It is hard to believe that it wasn't too long ago that movies didn't exist at all. Film is a great revelation for students to recognize. The genesis of movies, at least here in the U.S., began as a much different experience than it is today.

Thomas Edison is credited with bringing film to life here in the U.S. Edison's initial idea was that the experience of movie viewing should occur on an individual basis. His invention, the **Kinetoscope**, was a device through which customers could view moving images by looking in a peephole. Obviously, this presented a mere novelty. Picture a bunch of folks pushing each other out of the way to get a glimpse of the images displayed in this new invention.

It was actually a pair of brothers from France, Auguste and Louis Lumière, who really advanced the concept of film viewing closer to what we know it as today. Their invention involved both a camera and projector that made the display of their short films possible for a large audience. The Lumières' works are a great way to illustrate the evolution of camera technology and the genesis of **cinematography**. In particular, "The Arrival of a Train at La Ciotat" shows advancements in cinematographic **framing** by the inventive positioning of the camera. In this short, the Lumières decided to put the camera at an angle to the station platform, which helped create a depth unattainable if the camera were placed anywhere else.

George Méliès (1902), another filmmaker of the time, made *A Trip to the Moon*, which is a great example of one of the first **narrative** films. Here, unlike with the Lumières' first films, Méliès used editing to put his fantasy together. That, along with animation and special effects in the form of early trick shots, made *A Trip to the Moon* a groundbreaking short film, and one that should be viewed by any budding filmmaker.

Continue the discussion with students by sharing the story of the advent of photography. When it was invented in the mid-1830s, people thought it was cold, even vulgar, and certainly not art. Of course, it did not take long for them to get over the shock of it all; in fact, people were fascinated by it. The moving image was looked at in much the same way when it arrived. A quick search on the Internet can reveal so much of this history. If time permits, students could conduct a short historical research project on the evolution of film.

As you work through the chapters and assign in-class or independent viewings, you might also want to explore a great app available to Google Chrome called VideoNotes, which allows you to annotate a YouTube or other streaming video found online with notes that link to the time code of the clip. It also provides an environment for students to take notes on a video clip they are watching. You and your students can watch videos and take notes while it is playing on a split-screen interface. The great part of this program is that everything can be stored and saved and accessed from just about anywhere, and clicking on any one note that is entered and saved will take you directly to the related part of the video. For example, if you are watching a scene from *Close Encounters of The Third Kind* (Phillips, Phillips, & Spielberg, 1977; a great film) and want students to see a particular connection to one of the elements of a science fiction genre, you can pause the clip and enter a note for them to read. They, in turn, can also comment or do the same with a clip they are viewing.

After viewing some of the films suggested, discussing all that was seen, and again, placing that information on a board or in notes, a fun exercise for the class involves the creation of a moving image from simple still images. Figure 1.2 is an example of such an exercise.

THE BIG PICTURE . . . LITERALLY

The key to introducing this unit of instruction is to appeal to the variety of students' interest and to allow them to see the separate parts of filmmaking as a whole. They can then begin to recognize the diverse offerings that provide the elements for the films they are accustomed to and ones that they will be exposed to. The important thing at the onset is getting them excited. The following sections of this chapter offer a list of the main contributors to the film process, with activities developed to appeal to and guide student interest. The culminating exercise involves a viewing analysis. Recall that each student may have already completed the Interest-a-Lyzer, provided in

FUN WITH THE MOVING IMAGE

Students are to make a flipbook of about 30–40 images. Each student is to decide on a simple action idea (e.g., ball bouncing, horse running, man walking, etc.). By drawing a slight change in the action on each paper, the students will create the illusion of movement. The goal is for the students to see that there really isn't a moving image, only the appearance of one.

Materials Needed: Paper (Post-it pads work great), scissors, pencils, stapler.

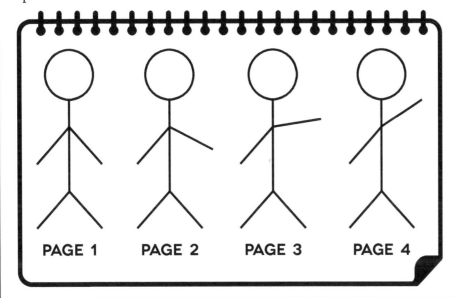

PAGE 1   PAGE 2   PAGE 3   PAGE 4

FIGURE 1.2. SAMPLE MOVING IMAGE EXERCISE.

Appendix E, and you will have a greater understanding of their interests as they relate to the discipline.

Every film has a process, whether it's an independent film, a blockbuster, a documentary, or an experimental film. Each has a specific set of steps to follow. All films begin with an idea. From this idea a script is born, and from there a film is made. The skills involved in filmmaking carry over into any field, but each is unique in its own way. The wise student will eventually ask about shooting without a script. Is this possible? Yes. Jean-Luc Godard did. But his scripts were born as visions. He knew the outcome. He had a mental script. He created art in a different way, as only a masterful artist can. Godard did start as your students will, though—as a beginner. From there, the possibilities are endless.

The information in the next section can be used for a brainstorming session, web activity, lecture, or handout. It is important for you to prepare by reading over the materials so that class discussions can be productive. All of the roles carry with them a specific set of skills that are as varied as your students'. There is truly something for everyone. Some jobs require more organized students. Others appeal to those who enjoy math. There are jobs for leaders and the highly creative. There are roles for the tech-savvy students and those for the artsy ones.

THE FILMMAKING PROCESS

There are three stages to the production process, and they can be broken down as such: **preproduction**, **production**, and **postproduction**.

PREPRODUCTION

Preproduction involves coming up with a solid idea, turning that idea into a script, storyboarding, scouting locations, hiring actors and crew, and of course, coming up with the funds to support a project. The main people involved at this stage are the screenwriter and the producer. The screenwriter's job is to write the script. The script may be either an original idea or an adapted piece. Screenwriters are some of the best researchers. Sometimes a screenwriter is hired by the producer to write a screenplay to a sequel for a popular franchise or to rework a screenplay in trouble.

The producer's main roles are to secure funds to support the project and to hire a director. A director then receives the script and is asked for his or her thoughts and overall "vision." The director will be the one in charge of all aspects of the filming process. It is his or her "eye" that we see. After this information is presented, engage the students in the exercise shown in Figure 1.3.

PRODUCTION

Production involves everything needed during the actual filming. Once the preparation stage is more or less complete, shooting can begin. When directors begin to shoot, it is important that they have with them a script, storyboards, and especially a production breakdown report (PBR; one is provided in Appendix D). Production breakdown reports are essential to the organization of the production stage. Valuable information like equipment, cast, location, props, and costumes are planned out beforehand and written into the PBRs. It is also common to bring a notebook and something to write with on each shoot. Directors often take notes as they shoot on anything

EXERCISE: THE PITCH SESSION

Screen the "pitch session" clip from Robert Altman's *The Player** (Brown, Tolkin, Wechsler, & Altman, 1992). It is the opening scene, which begins with an excellent establishing shot, completed in one take.

Here aspiring and working screenwriters pitch their ideas to the producer. The idea is to catch his attention in as few words as possible. Have the students discuss which "pitchers" are successful. How do they take different approaches to get their idea across?

Next, have the students create their own pitch session, where you will act as producer. The students pitch their ideas to you (and possibly the class)—again, the key is that they are concise and creative, expressing their idea in 25–30 words.

FIGURE 1.3. PITCH SESSION EXERCISE.

from costumes, to hair and makeup, lighting, and the overall experience (i.e., what works, what doesn't, etc).

The director and the producer need some assistance, so there are assistant directors and production assistants. They keep everyone on track and on schedule. Responsibility is key! We also see the appearance of lighting, electrical, and sound engineers. All of the lights that grace the set, the power needed, and the recording devices are tools of the gaffers and grips, who set up the lighting. Gaffers and grips have some assistants, too, known as best boys, who carry everything.

Cinematographers, or more commonly known as directors of photography, shoot the actual footage being filmed. They know the cameras, they know the light, and so they capture what the director envisioned. Quite often, there are a secondary group of camera folks that shoot footage of things related to the areas being filmed. This is called **B-roll**. These shots may be landscapes, buildings, streets, and any other static elements.

In sound, there are the folks who hold the microphone when a scene is being shot. They are the boom operators, who, in working with the sound engineer, record everything that is said or heard. They may also record some baseline sound or ambient noise.

Actors are the people who perform the roles in the script and have had some time to prepare for production. Prior to filming, they have auditioned for roles and were selected for their ability to capture the director and screenwriters' vision. The actors would just be voices if not for makeup artists, costume designers, and hairdressers. These jobs often coordinate to capture the look and "feel" of the character. For more tips on the shooting stage, refer to Chapter 5.

KEY TERM
- **B-roll:** supplemental footage in a documentary that is intercut into the main footage (e.g., landscapes, buildings, etc.)

POSTPRODUCTION

The final stage of production is called postproduction, or in industry terms, post. Anything and everything done to the footage after production is considered postproduction. This includes film and sound editing, special effects, and score and soundtrack. In fact, most of the sound we hear in the final cut of a film is not the sound recorded during filming, including characters' dialogue. Sound editors and foley artists work very hard layering and combining sound to aid in the overall aural experience of the viewer. With automated dialogue replacement (ADR), actors go in to a sound booth and rerecord their dialogue for higher quality sound. It's the sound editor's job to sync it all up.

Once every scene is shot and a "wrap" is called, it is the editor's job to piece together all of the footage in a way that also adheres to the script and storyboard vision. The editor works in close contact with the director, selecting angles of the same shot and blending transitions and cuts in a precise and deliberate way.

The sound editors and designers add the soundtrack. They use existing sounds and may add up to 50 or more "tracks" on a single shot. These can be effects, enhancements, or even rerecorded vocals, done by the actors if the dialogue is not audible. Foley artists may be called in to add sounds that they create themselves, such as doors closing, feet walking, and glass breaking.

Special effects artists utilize technology to create **computer-generated imagery** (CGI) or live-action effects, such as car chases or large explosions. Composers work to write, compose, and conduct the musical score for a film, keeping in mind the mood and theme of the scene and overall film. This score may be strictly conducted by the composer or may also include prerecorded songs from popular or new artists. For more tips on the assembly stage, refer to Chapter 6. Table 1.1 is a list of positions and jobs involved in the filmmaking process, along with a brief description of duties. Figure 1.4 illustrates the hierarchy of film production.

TABLE 1.1
POSITIONS AND JOBS IN FILMMAKING PROCESS

Producer: Fundraises, hires key personnel, and arranges for distributors. The producer is involved throughout all phases of the filmmaking process, from development to completion of a project.
Casting Director: Works closely with the director to cast the film
Director: The "general." Hires cast and crew; in charge of overall look and feel of the film
First Assistant Director: Organizes the crew, secures equipment, and maintains shooting schedule
Script Supervisor: Maintains a daily log of the shots covered and their relation to the script during the course of a production
Publicist: Works to publicize and promote the film during all phases of production
Production Designer: Develops, coordinates, facilitates, and oversees the overall design of the production (i.e., anything that will appear in front of the camera)
Art Director: Develops, coordinates, facilitates, and oversees the design of the sets, whether onstage or practical locations
Key Makeup Person: Applies and maintains the cast's makeup
Key Hairdresser: Dresses and maintains the cast's hair
Costume Designer: Designs, obtains, assembles, and maintains the costumes for a production.
Property Manager: Gathers, maintains, and manages all the props for a production.
Set Decorator: Dresses and decorates the sets: painting, draping, arranging props, and small-scale landscaping
Director of Photography, aka, DP or Cinematographer: The camera and lighting supervisor in charge of the visual look and design of the entire movie
Gaffer: Sometimes called the lighting designer, the gaffer is the chief electrician who supervises set lighting
Best-Boy Electric: The chief assistant to the gaffer in the lighting of sets and the operation of electrical systems
Electrician: Works under the direction of the gaffer in the lighting of sets and the operation of electrical systems
Mixer/Recordist: The on-set/on-location sound engineer responsible for the recording of production sound and any sync-related, on-set sound mixing and playback

TABLE 1.1, CONTINUED

Boom Operators: Hold microphone booms and cables, place microphones, and operate various recording devices

Key Grip: Works with the gaffer in setting and cutting lights to create shadow effects for the set lighting. Supervises camera cranes, dollies, etc.

Best-Boy Grip: The chief assistant to the key grip, aiding him or her in rigging, cutting light, and carrying out camera movements

Dolly Grip: The chief grip responsible for operating the camera dolly, usually in conjunction with the best-boy grip

Editor: Assembles the film until a final cut is reached; in charge of color correction and other post-production effects

Assistant Editor: Logs and captures footage, organizing and managing media in coordination with the script supervisor's log

Sound Designer, aka, Sound Editor: Responsible for the creation of the overall soundtrack of the film. The sound designer supervises the mix of music, dialogue, ADR, Foley, and sound effects.

Composer: Writes original music to be heard in the film, both diegetic and nondiegetic

Foley Artist: Creates sound effects to accompany specific visual objects, movements, and sound sources, such as footsteps or punches

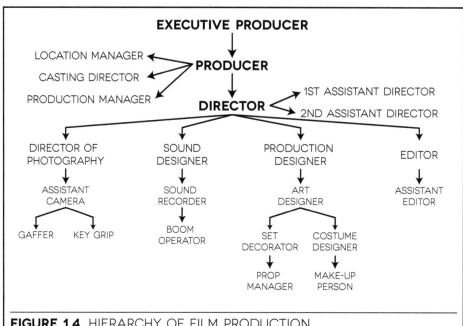

FIGURE 1.4. HIERARCHY OF FILM PRODUCTION.

Once all of the components of the filmmaking process have been introduced and discussed, it is beneficial to watch a film, or selections from a film, that depicts the process of moviemaking in action. This allows students to recognize and comment on a variety of elements that occur during filmmaking. *Singin' in the Rain* (Freed, Kelly, & Donen, 1952) is an excellent film for students to see the production process at work. Use the study guide below to generate a conversation about what they see.

The following list of suggested films also helps to illustrate the filmmaking process covered in this chapter. They are ordered by age rating, beginning with the most appropriate and moving to more advanced content: You will find similar lists accompanying each of the feature film study guides.

- 🎬 *Hugo* (King, Headington, Depp, & Scorsese, 2011)
- 🎬 *Super 8* (Burk, Spielberg, & Abrams, 2011)
- 🎬 *Shadow of the Vampire* (Cage, Levine, & Merhige, 2000)
- 🎬 *Day for Night* (Berbert & Truffaut, 1973)

STUDY GUIDE
SINGIN' IN THE RAIN

Note: Direction, production, and acting credits for this film can be found at http://www.imdb.com/title/tt0045152/?ref_=nv_sr_1.

1. Which steps of the film production process are shown in *Singin' in the Rain*? Give an example of a scene from the film that shows each step.

2. Besides actors and actresses, which members of the production crew do we see in action?

3. An interesting part of *Singin' in the Rain* is that it is a film that shows how a film gets made. Some of the props seen on screen are actually pieces of equipment that are also used in the shooting and editing processes. Make a list of all of the filmmaking equipment you see.

ASSESSING OTHER STUDENT FILMS

At this point, it could be beneficial for students to watch films produced by other middle and high school students and have the students comment on a variety of perspectives and elements. Even though this is early on in the process, it will help to have them see the big "little" pictures first. Rest assured that at the end of the unit, when we work with the final assignment, the answers to the questions in Handout 1.1 will be radically different. This first assignment will serve as a marker of students' progress and understanding.

You will be able to find short student films by conducting a quick Internet search. As you work to complete projects with your students annually, you will begin to amass a catalogue of your own student films. This will be beneficial because your students will see films made with the same equipment and tools they have to work with.

Suggested sites for viewing student work are:

- 🎬 Short of the Week's Best Student Films: http://www.shortoftheweek. com/category/collection/student-films/
- 🎬 Beacon Charter High School's Student Film Page: http://vimeo.com/ user2006081

Use Handout 1.1: Looking and Learning Exercise to engage students in the process of reading a student film. This is a very basic start—feel free to adapt it to suit your class. It can also be used during the screening of other films.

HANDOUT 1.1
LOOKING AND LEARNING EXERCISE

Film Analysis: _____

Film Title: _____

Directed by: _____

Note to students: Consider the following elements when completing this handout: script, locations, sets and props, wardrobe, lighting, sound, camera angles, actors, makeup, hair style, edits, visual effects, sound effects, musical score, audio tracks.

1. What do you think is the theme or message of the film?

   _____

   _____

   _____

2. How does the director convey that message? Explain.

   _____

   _____

   _____

3. Describe the technical aspects of the production (e.g., camera work, editing, etc.).

   _____

   _____

   _____

4. What are the strengths of the production?

   _____

   _____

   _____

5. What are its weaknesses?

   _____

   _____

   _____

6. If you were given the task of remaking this film, what would you do differently? Explain.

   _____

   _____

   _____

CHAPTER 2

MISE-EN-SCÈNE
WHY WE SEE WHAT WE SEE

The first important step in teaching **mise-en-scène** is for you and your students to learn the proper pronunciation of the term. Say it aloud to them, "meez-on-sen." Now that you have that out of the way, let's move forward with the confidence needed to define and explain the film technique's many intricacies. In many ways, studying mise-en-scène will help your students begin to pull apart the many facets of the filmmaking process by beginning to see production through the director's eyes.

In simple terms, mise-en-scène is everything the director chooses to be filmed. This includes choices about setting, lighting, costume/makeup, and staging and figure gesture (i.e., where the characters are and what they are doing). A main point that needs to be addressed at the onset of this introduction is that all films have mise-en-scène. This includes documentary and animated films. It is a common assumption among students that first begin to study this film technique that only some films use "it." Explaining to them that mise-en-scène relates to the meaning that the audience gleans from watching the film, not the actual technique itself, can clear up the confusion.

The choices the director makes have direct consequence on the audience, whether they know it or not. Mise-en-scène is not simply the background or clothes or movement. It has the power to cue

KEY TERM
- Mise-en-scène: all the elements placed in front of the camera to be filmed; this includes the setting and props, lighting, costumes, makeup, and figure behavior

the viewer to the mood and intentions of the characters, define personality traits, and foreshadow plot elements yet to come. Mise-en-scène helps define **genre** as well. Genre is a term that signifies a particular type or category of literature or art; it is how we classify and identify different types of movies. What would a Western be without cowboy hats and chaps, Native American headdresses, horses, guns and arrows, mining towns, saloons, the prairie, the desert, and the mountains? These are all elements of mise-en-scène.

There are four general aspects of mise-en-scène: setting, costume and makeup, lighting, and staging and figure gesture. Setting is not only *where* the film takes place, but also *when* the events take place. Creating a realistic time period for a film is just as important as the physical setting of the film. For example, you typically wouldn't see someone driving a Toyota Prius in a classic film noir. In choosing where to shoot, the director must decide between filming on location or on set. On location involves taking the cast and crew to a place other than the confines of a film studio or back lot, which is known as a "set." Of course, if an entire film, or even some scenes, take place in New York City, some filmmakers go for authenticity and shoot in New York. Others, for many reasons, decide to shoot on location in another city but use effects and camera angles to create the idea and look of New York. Still, there are others who opt to build their own New York on a set in a film studio. In actuality, many films are shot using a combination of these options to create the milieu, the setting where something occurs. Whichever they choose, directors know that setting is not simply a background that the actors perform in front of. The right setting can convey a state of mind, mood, and feeling. Choices of color, shape, and texture, as they relate to costumes, lighting, building design, and materials, are all crucial in creating the proper setting for a film.

Like setting, costume design and style have many important functions in the overall film. The director's choices on costume come down to color, texture, shape, and flexibility, for even the tightness and looseness of a character's clothing can convey meaning. A character wearing dark sunglasses might elicit a deeper meaning for the viewer. Similarly, the right costume can provide details of a time period or present a commentary on the characters, suggesting or revealing essential aspects of their personalities or function in the story. Makeup works in quite the same way. In early cinema, makeup was needed because actors' faces would disappear when the film stocks were developed. Nowadays it is used to enhance the appearance of the actors on screen and cover up blemishes. Everyone onscreen wears some amount of makeup. Makeup becomes even more important when found in certain genres like horror and science fiction, where makeup artists are challenged to create realistic effects and fantastical characters.

Lighting is probably the most overlooked aspect of mise-en-scène. It is more than just flipping a switch on or off. Lighting works to guide the audience's attention to important details or to hide particular elements from them. Lighting is defined by its strength (hard or soft), its source (where in the frame the light comes from and enters), and by the shadows and color created. A creative lighting design can alter a film in dramatic ways. Likewise, a good film can easily be ruined with bad lighting.

The fourth and final aspect of mise-en-scène has two categories: staging and figure gesture. Staging refers to the placement of objects in the frame, and figure gesture refers to movement and performance. The term *figure* does not only apply to human characters, but also covers animals, robots, and even inanimate objects, like a clock or statue. The director meticulously controls the placement and movement of all of the objects in the scene. In many ways, a single film shot resembles a painting or photograph, the major difference being that a movie's frame has no boundaries; anything can enter the frame at any time and change the meaning of the image. A painting or photograph has boundaries that are clearly defined and finite; nothing exists outside of the frame.

All of these elements must be carefully planned out before filming begins. The director's power over mise-en-scène controls not only what we see but when we see it and for how long. Elements of mise-en-scène that are left onscreen longer are probably more important—the director wants to make sure we see it, wonder about its significance, and then generate some meaning from it.

FIGURE 2.1. EXAMPLE OF WELL-CONSTRUCTED STAGING FROM ORSON WELLES'S (1941) *CITIZEN KANE*. THE PLACING OF THE CHARACTERS IN THE FRAME GIVES INSIGHT INTO EACH CHARACTER'S IMPORTANCE.

TABLEAU EXERCISE

The elements of mise-en-scène also work together to create a meaningful and believable world onscreen, and as your students work through the following exercise, they will begin to see how each of the elements are important to the overall film.

It would be helpful if you could provide a still image from a film in different genres to be used during the following exercise. A simple Internet search for "examples of [genre type]" will uncover a host of images that can be used during class discussion. You can also find movie stills at http://www.imdb.com. This exercise will also offer the opportunity for you to become more familiar with the genre types covered.

Begin by cutting out the provided genre cards in Handout 2.1. Feel free to create your own on any type of medium. Then, divide the class into smaller groups and randomly assign one of the genre cards to each group. The groups can then be instructed to create a "scene" using each of the four elements of mise-en-scène. Note that there will not be actual filming at this point, or even acting or dialogue. Students are simply creating a frozen picture, or **tableau**, a "still" image that successfully uses mise-en-scène to define the genre.

During class, the groups should research the assigned genre in books or web links provided by you. As students begin to list the elements needed for each of their genres in the four areas of mise-en-scène, they should also discuss what they will need to round up and bring in to class to set up the scene. In fact, it would help if the lists were posted on a board so that the students could contribute to others' lists. Homework requires the students to collect items that need to be brought in for the next meeting.

When students return to class with their materials, they should be given a space to work in and enough time to discuss and set up their scene. If need be, lighting elements can be created with simple desk lamps, small floodlights, or more professional lighting rigs. Flashlights work well, too. Some students may bring in a source for lighting, but it helps if you can provide a variety of light sources. A simple call-out to your entire faculty could result in a wealth of lighting sources. Depending on the setting of the class or room to be used, the students will have to go with what they have to work with. If weather and time permit, groups could also use an outside space close to the classroom. This exercise can be as elaborate as you want!

Once groups have been given enough time to set up (e.g., costumes, props, figures, makeup, and lighting), announce for everyone to stay in their positions so that you can take a digital photo of the scene. These photos can then be printed out, projected on a wall or screen, or posted to a webpage for further viewing, discussion, and evaluation.

When all group work has been documented, it is important for the entire class to view each of the six genre images that were covered in the exercise. A simple follow-up exercise would involve assigning each of the photos to different groups and having the students identify as many elements of mise-en-scène as they can. A more in-depth exercise would be for individual students or groups to analyze each of the remaining images, possibly critiquing and peer evaluating. Remember, the more students start to develop the language and understanding of the elements of mise-en-scène in as many genres as possible, the better they will become at understanding what will be covered in the following chapters.

A NOTE ABOUT MOTIF

The earliest forms of storytelling relied on motifs to draw connections and generate meaning throughout a narrative. Film presents the same association. Developing patterns, recurring characters, lines of repeated dialogue, and repeated colors all help transform a film into an enjoyable and meaningful event for the audience. A **motif** is anything in a film that is significantly repeated. Every film contains narrative and visual devices, but the audience's role is to distinguish between what's important and what's not. A desk that helps define a room as an office is certainly essential to the definition of the setting, but the desk is only a desk. It does not offer any deeper meaning than that. If, however, that same desk carries multiple functions throughout the film, then we have a motif. For example, the lighter in Alfred Hitchcock's (1951) *Strangers on a Train* is a simple prop that holds significant meaning and multiple functions. On the surface, it is just a lighter. But it also connects the characters of Guy to Anne, Bruno to Guy, and Guy to the murder of Miriam. *Note:* You should really check out this film if you haven't already. There is much to learn from Hitchcock!

Another way to demonstrate this repetition, without having to screen an entire film, would be to show the shower scene from Hitchcock's (1960) *Psycho*. During this scene, the shower curtain has multiple functions. On the surface it is just a shower curtain, something to stop water from getting onto the bathroom floor. But it also functions to obscure the "Mother" from view as "she" enters the bathroom, facilitates Marion's death grip, and becomes a tool for Norman to use to wrap the body.

The study guide below has questions intended to guide the students in explaining important detail about *Singin' in the Rain* (Freed, Kelly, & Donen,

1952), which was explored in the previous chapter. These questions can be used as homework, classwork, or just thought-provoking discussion points. They are also intended to provide a template for use with other films that could be chosen for a screening. A little adaptation goes a long way. Other suggested screenings for this chapter include:

- Beginner: *Strangers on a Train* (Hitchcock, 1951)
- Intermediate: *Edward Scissorhands* (Di Novi & Burton, 1990)
- Advanced: *The Rules of the Game* (Renoir, Jay, & Renoir, 1939)

STUDY GUIDE
MOTIF IN *SINGIN' IN THE RAIN*

1. Can you isolate any motifs in the film? How do these visual patterns function or play out across the film?

2. Identify examples from the film where the mise-en-scène really stands out. How does the mise-en-scène contribute to the film's meaning? How does the mise-en-scène evoke mood and/or emotion?

Name: _____ Date: _____

GENRE CARDS

WESTERN	MUSICAL
SCIENCE FICTION	FILM NOIR
HORROR	THRILLER

BONUS CARDS FOR ADVANCED PROJECTS

1950s MELODRAMA	ITALIAN NEOREALISM
THE BRAT PACK/ JOHN HUGHES ERA	THE SILENT ERA

CHAPTER 3

ALL THE PRETTY GENRES

KEY TERMS

- **Genre:** the type or classification of films recognized by their familiar conventions
- **Subgenres:** a more specific way of defining and categorizing types of films

Coming off the heels of the previous chapter, it is beneficial to begin a conversation about genre, or the categories that movies fall into. Although there are a host of other genres, subgenres, and branches, the focus here is to explore four particular genres in depth: the Western, musical, film noir, and science fiction. Through these, we will focus on the six conventions that define a genre: story formula, theme, presentation, character types, setting, and stars. We'll also look at how genres have influenced the art of storytelling. The overarching theme of this series of exercises revolves around the question: How do we define and distinguish genre?

The term **genre** originates from the French, meaning "kind" or "type." Ever since the birth of cinema, films have been classified by genre. At a time when video stores were still as prevalent as fast food joints, you could explore sections classified by genre. The modern movie hubs Netflix, Hulu Plus, and others offer searches in this way. Basically, it is important to note that some students will already have an understanding of genre.

Within each of the genres we explore, there is further classification used to explain the type of movie actually being watched. The term comedy doesn't quite do it, so the terms slapstick, grossout, romantic, parody, mockumentary, buddy picture, and more are used, all **subgenres** of comedy that more precisely describe what the films are like. Over the decades, and since the beginning of cinema, genres have often been mixed and combined to create hybrid genres. For example, *Oklahoma!* is both a Western and a musical. The chart in Figure 3.1 might help to further categorize many different genres. It is not an exhaustive list, but it does name many of the major genres present in movies today.

DEFINING A GENRE

Like any other exercise in this text, it is important to let your own interests and appreciation guide the discussions you have and the lessons you teach. This guide is meant to define that which you already have experienced and recognized in your career as a film watcher. Always start with what you know.

Each and every film possesses a certain type of defining characteristics. Musicals are distinct because singing and dancing can occur at any moment, in any situation. Science fiction films use futuristic technology and time travel. The Western is unique in its setting (and is the only genre named after its setting). Film noir is often defined by its character types and lighting style, among other things. In theory, we can look at any movie and pick out similar elements that help define its place in a particular genre.

Let us look briefly at the elements present in genres. **Story formula** refers to the film's **narrative**, or story. **Themes** are broad concepts that offer deeper meaning or insight in understanding the film. This is usually intentional and attributed to the director. **Character type** refers to distinct character traits—hero, villain, antihero. **Setting** refers not only to where a movie's action takes place, but also to when it takes place (e.g., Hill Valley, CA, 1985). **Presentation** involves the cinematic language of a film, or what is known as the film's form. This includes camera angles, editing choices, sound, lighting, and much more. **Stars** are the actors we associate with a particular genre, such as Dwayne Johnson for action films, Will Ferrell for comedy, and Nicolas Cage with basically anything he's asked to do. Once you begin to understand how a particular genre is defined, you can view just about any film and begin to dissect the elements you recognize for a specific genre.

It is important to note that with each genre type, a variety of avenues for class discussion, assigning work, and general introductions to one or more genres can be taken. The ideal situation involves all of the students learning each of the suggested genres. Although they will retain the information related to the elements of genre, they will also become well versed in the specific types. If time presents an issue, students could self-select into one

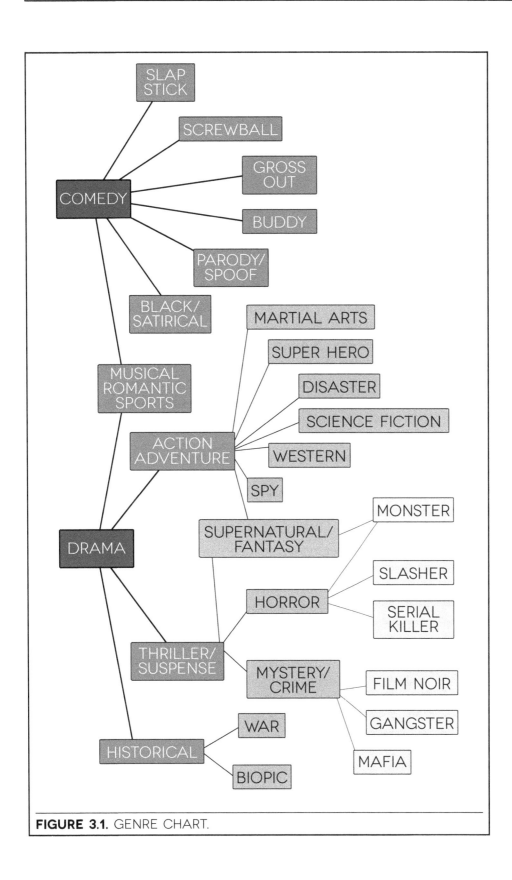

FIGURE 3.1. GENRE CHART.

KEY TERM

- **Movie trailer:** a short montage intended to promote an upcoming movie release. The term "trailer" is used because trailers used to be shown after the feature in theaters

of many groups and explore the elements of genre through the lens of a specific genre. It is our belief that classroom discussion is crucial during the introduction of genre. Students should share as much as they can within their groups and to the rest of the class. The more your students speak about what they notice and discover, the more they will become familiar with each of the genre types, recognizing them on their own when watching a movie. Table 3.1 presents a look at four genres in terms of their elements. This graphic can be used as a jumping-off point for many small activities. Each of the elements is presented as a question, and there is a suggested viewing category for each of them. Even if you do not have access to the entire film, clips of each can be found online and will prove helpful in defining the genre for your students.

The first activity involves a simple Internet or newspaper search. Try to collect a few issues of the local or national paper and save the arts/life/ entertainment sections. A Friday or weekend edition works best, as it has all of the new release movies listed. *The New York Times* even displays full-page ads for new movies. If newspapers are a thing of the past for you, visits to the homepages of local cinemas or sites like http://www.fandango.com or http://www.rottentomatoes.com can yield a great collection of the most current films. Whatever method you choose, the key is to have a wealth of titles to choose from.

Once the posters are cut out of the newspaper or printed from the web, have the students look up the synopsis of each of the films, making note of what genre the film falls into. An added element to this search would be to have the students watch the **movie trailer**, or preview. A great resource is The Internet Movie Data Base at http://www.imdb.com, a complete database of just about every movie ever made. Students can access movie specs, production information, movie stills (photos), posters, and trailers. This resource can prove quite valuable throughout the remainder of the text. Students can then organize the list of movies into genres and describe how the movie posters and trailers inform the audience about their specific genres.

If time permits, and I really hope it does, present the YouTube video, "Scary Mary" (https://www.youtube.com/watch?v=2T5_0AGdFic), to your students. In short, a very creative individual took select clips from the classic, *Mary Poppins* (Disney & Stevenson, 1964), and edited them together with the addition of new soundtrack elements, producing a trailer for a horror movie. This single screening of a one-minute video can open students' eyes to what genre really means.

At some point, it is important for the students to view actual scenes from some films in different genres. See Table 3.1 for recommendations. The goal is for students to pick out the elements of a specific genre while watching a film. A more guided viewing, where you can pause, rewind, and rewatch a

TABLE 3.1
GENRE ELEMENTS

	Western	Horror	Science Fiction	Film Noir
Story Formula: What can you expect to happen?	Goal-driven characters on a journey; good versus evil	Hero must "win" in the end by defeating evil	Protecting/ saving the universe; space exploration; time travel	Crime committed; often told in flashback
Themes: What is the filmmaker trying to say?	Civilization versus wilderness; White versus Other	Good versus evil; questioning the existence of the supernatural or paranormal	Creation of the universe; social, political, and philosophical issues	Sin, morals, and ethics
Character Types: Who can you expect to appear as characters?	White hero; cowboys; Indians; gunslingers; townspeople	Hero—man or "final" girl; villain—monster, killer, supernatural beings	Scientists/ mad scientist; time travelers; space aliens; robots, androids, cyborgs	Male protagonist caught up in the crime; femme fatale or spiderwoman; good girl; detectives
Setting: Where and when is the story taking place?	The West—desert, prairies, mountains; Monument Valley	Small towns; isolated areas; "haunted" places	Outer space; the future; alternate universe/reality	Night; 1930s and 40s; urban; dark
Presentation: What cinematic elements are being used?	Extreme long shots—the landscape dominates; costumes and props	High and low angles; "Dutch" angle; POV shots; sound effects; tension created through editing	Special effects; futuristic technology	Venetian blind lighting; dark shadows; smoke, rain
Stars: Actors and directors associated with the genre	John Wayne, Clint Eastwood, John Ford	Jamie Lee Curtis, Boris Karloff, Wes Craven, John Carpenter	Arnold Schwarzenegger, Keanu Reeves, George Lucas, Stephen Spielberg	Humphrey Bogart, James Cagney, Billy Wilder, John Huston, Lauren Bacall
Suggested Viewing	*The Searchers, High Noon, Unforgiven, True Grit*	Classic monster movies (*Dracula, Frankenstein*), *Fright Night, Nosferatu*	*Star Wars, Back to the Future, E.T., The Matrix*	*Double Indemnity, The Maltese Falcon, The Big Sleep*

particular scene or scenes, provides the best method. Students could also be asked to work independently, either taking their own notes, or filling in a blank chart supplied by you. They could also be grouped with others who share a similar interest in genre and assigned different elements to watch for. If you do not have the means to access the entire film, either through Netflix, another streaming site, or on a purchased DVD, you can search for clips online through YouTube, Vimeo, and other sites.

An assignment or follow-up homework involves the independent viewing of a film in a group's chosen genre. They could submit a written analysis to you, present their analysis to the class, or add them to a class file folder intended to be accessed by members of the class seeking films to watch. This could also be completed as an essay assignment, a film review, or by filling out answers to a questionnaire.

The study guide questions below are designed to be answered after a screening of John Ford's *The Searchers* (Whitney & Ford, 1956), but can be adapted to any film from any genre. As a finale to this section, we have gone a step further in defining with detail the specifics of each of the elements of the Western genre. *The Searchers* is a classic Western because the director uses the common six criteria known to be standard in the genre.

STUDY GUIDE
THE SEARCHERS

1. How does mise-en-scène (i.e., setting, lighting, costume, and behavior of characters and objects) help define genre? Which specific elements of mise-en-scène make *The Searchers* a Western?
2. Are there any other film techniques that also help identify a genre?
3. After watching *The Searchers*, does it match your expectations of a Western? Explain your answer.
4. We have always associated certain stars with certain genres. John Wayne is no exception; his exaggerated acting style is very distinguished him throughout his career. Think about his performance in *The Searchers*. In what ways is Wayne ideally suited for this role?

Again, you could use this model as a template for classroom assignments where students could complete a similar exercise for each of the genres. Students, having studied one or more of the genres during class could be asked to complete a similar task for each of the remaining genres, or the genres they want to focus on. The information could be used to create "genre posters" for the class, which could be displayed and used for reference later on. A sample genre poster for Westerns is modeled in Figure 3.3.

THE WESTERN AND THE SIX GENRE CONVENTIONS

Most Westerns are fast-paced action stories chock full of things like gun fights, robberies, holdups, runaway stagecoaches, shoot-outs, showdowns, stampedes, barroom brawls, and more. The stories are also interesting because of conflicts that arise. The main characters are typically goal-oriented men who set out on a journey; their main goal is to maintain law and order. Along the way, they are faced with challenges that hinder the progress of achieving their goals. These conflicts show themselves in many different ways, but most commonly in the classic archetypal conflict: good versus evil.

In *The Searchers*, Uncle Ethan (John Wayne) returns to his family's home right before there is an attack by the Comanche Indians, led by the main villain, Scar (Henry Brandon). This attack sets off a series of events that are based around Ethan, with the help of his half-White/half-Indian adopted nephew, Martin (Jeffrey Hunter). They search for his niece, Debbie (Natalie Wood), who has been abducted by Scar. This follows the goal-oriented story formula, as Ethan's main goal is to find Debbie and bring her home. Problems arise, however, when Ethan and Martin finally find Debbie. She has been taken as one of Scar's wives and now speaks Comanche and dresses in traditional Native American garb. This poses a problem for Ethan, as his hatred (and on many levels, his racism) for any non-Whites supersedes his desire to save his niece. Ethan no longer sees Debbie as White. Therefore, his goal has now shifted from saving Debbie by bringing her home to saving Debbie by destroying (i.e., killing) her.

The good versus evil archetype is a bit more complex after further thought. Ethan is meant to be the hero and represent good but he has a dark past, as evidenced by the way he arrives home with secrets and a pouch of freshly minted coins. On the other hand, Scar is meant to be perceived as evil, based purely on the classic archetype—he is Native American. He does commit violent and terrible acts, burning down villages and abducting people; however, the film reveals his motives as being revenge driven. By other means, his actions are a reaction to what the White man has done to his family. These themes dig deep into each man's character and further complicate the conflict. Classically, Ethan is good and Scar is bad, based purely on race. But in this film, John Ford challenges that thinking by villainizing Ethan and humanizing Scar.

Nearly all Westerns share common themes that become evident by reading deeper into the film. Central to many of these films is the conflict between civilization and wilderness. An outside force is threatening the main character's world. In some cases, that force is represented by Native Americans. The most widely used conflict is Whites versus Native Americans. The Native Americans in these films are inhumanely portrayed as savages—uneducated, uncivilized, violent animals, and it's the White hero's job to restore order. These themes present themselves in *The Searchers*. Scar and his tribe represent the outside force threatening civilization, Ethan and his family. The setting also represents the wilderness as Ethan and Martin battle the elements (e.g., snow and cold, hot desert sun, etc.) in their 10-year search for Debbie. Of course, the White versus Other theme is in full force here as well.

Looking at any Western, you'll be able to notice similar characters from film to film. The main character of a typical Western is a rugged White hero. He's a man of action,

---

FIGURE 3.3. WESTERN GENRE CONVENTIONS.

not words, and it's his job to ride into town and restore order. Other character types in Westerns include: lawmen (as antagonists or protagonists, often a former outlaw or gunslinger), cowboys and Indians, the cunning gambler, the sidekick, the town drunk, and the settler.

Female characters are usually either schoolmarms or prostitutes. The prostitutes long for a better life and look for a way out while schoolmarms are educated and cultured, yet are irresistibly drawn to bad men and the violence that surrounds them. Ethan represents the White hero in *The Searchers*; even though he has a dark past and at one point tries to kill Debbie, his goal to restore order to what's left of his family and desire to do what's right at any cost are representative of what makes up a true Western hero. Scar clearly represents the villain in this film. However, as mentioned, he also has reasons for his actions. Martin is Ethan's sidekick, and Laurie is the educated woman who is attracted to a man who represents the unknown, Martin. The same goes for Ethan's sister-in-law, but that's a whole other can of worms!

The Western is the only genre named after its setting, so that's got to be important! Most classic Westerns take place in the 1880s and 1890s, but the "West" is not necessarily a particular place. The genre may be set on the prairie, in the mountains, or in the desert. But whatever the setting, the landscape is a dominant visual and thematic element. The wide-open spaces of the deserts, prairies, and mountains are used to symbolize that anything can happen, good or bad. The setting of *The Searchers* is Monument Valley, one of John Ford's favorite film locations. Nothing historically important happened here, but it sure looks pretty! The wide-open spaces and desert are iconic images of the Western.

Many genres also feature certain elements of cinematic language that communicate tone and atmosphere. This is what is referred to as presentation. Westerns, a genre clearly associated with setting, feature a great many exterior shots that juxtapose the characters with the environment they inhibit. The human subject tends to dominate the frame in most movie compositions, but many of the Western exterior shots are framed so that the "civilized" characters are dwarfed by the overwhelming expanse of wilderness around them. This helps add to the theme of civilization versus wilderness by putting so much emphasis on the wilderness. Other aspects of mise-en-scène also help to define the genre, especially costumes and props. What would the Western be without the hats, chaps, guns and horses?

We associate certain stars with different genres. This has a lot to do with typecasting, yes, but also it is a function of early Hollywood contractual obligations. In the early days, actors would sign long contracts with film studios and if a film did well, the studio would crank out countless other similar films, often using the same actors. To a certain extent the same is true today. Think of all the Will Ferrell comedy movies. John Wayne is forever associated with the Western. In nearly 150 films, Wayne starred in over 75 westerns. This is even more interesting when you consider that John Wayne is a character created by a film studio, not a real person. The actor Marion Robert Morrison took on the stage name John Wayne and created the character, how he looks, talks, and even walks, as a persona.

Although actors are usually what we associate genres to, directors can also be a factor. Some directors become so well known for working within certain genres that it's all we think about when their names come up. John Ford is forever associated with the Western. Many of the most beloved Westerns are his, including *Stagecoach*, *The Man Who Shot Liberty Valance*, *Rio Grande*, and of course, *The Searchers*.

FIGURE 3.3. CONTINUED.

CHAPTER 4

CRAFTING THE STORY

THE SCREENPLAY

Before every story becomes a film and reaches an audience, it begins as a screenplay, or script. Some scripts spawn from an original idea, and the screenwriter labors to create a working draft that will be used for filming. Other times, writers are hired by a production company to write a first draft, clean up an existing draft, or completely rewrite an entire script. However the idea originates, all scripts go through multiple drafts before filming begins. What follows is a broad look at screenwriting rules and tips for both you and your students.

It should be said at the onset that time constraints may shorten the training involved with having students write scripts for the screen, so you should do your best to introduce the very basics first. Start by picking a movie that you think they would be familiar with and print out an example of a script page or pages. That should be enough to introduce the important element of a screenplay. The breakfast scene on Tatooine from *Star Wars Episode IV: A New Hope* (Kurtz & Lucas, 1977) has been a favorite of mine for years and is easily found online. Try polling the class and see if the students can suggest ones to use. You can also access hundreds of scripts at the following websites:

- 🎬 http://www.scriptologist.com/Directory/Filmmaking/ Screenplays/screenplays.html and
- 🎬 http://www.script-o-rama.com/

When introducing the general principles of screenwriting to the class, it is helpful to cover the "rules" first to provide a good starting point for discussion and activity. Even though many scripts differ in their themes and styles, they all adhere to the following rules. First, a script is always written in the present tense, with the action presented to the reader as if it were happening now. Second, a script should stick to the facts, only concerned with what the audience will see and hear. Details about the background of characters should only be revealed in the action and/or dialogue. Never in a script are lines like the following:

> He is a worrying sort who was never loved by his mother.
> She is unlicensed and shouldn't be treating patients.

This is also extended to include what the characters are secretly thinking or plotting, unless it is dramatized through actions, dialogue, and visual context, for example:

> The Man is impatient and anxious to get back to work.
> He only pretends to pack up his belongings because he knows that as soon as the Park Ranger leaves, he can continue to camp.

Once these standard rules have been explained and understood, it is time to introduce the elements of a script. The following information could be written as a group activity that has students create a poster or website intended for the class to reference.

ELEMENTS OF A SCRIPT

SCENE HEADINGS

Scene headings are how the time and place of a scene is established. Each scene begins with a new scene header. If the action changes from day to night, a new scene is needed. If a scene changes from a bedroom to a living room, a new scene is needed. Even if a scene takes place in the same room, just hours later, a new scene header must be created to represent the time change.

The following is how a proper scene heading is built:

EXT. or INT.

Begin each scene heading with either exterior (EXT) or interior (INT). These are always abbreviated and let the reader/viewer know if the scene takes place indoors or out. This is also where the precise location is specified. There's no need to go into great detail here, but the writing must be specific enough so that anyone picking up the script will be able to understand where the scene takes place. So start with something like this:

EXT. DOWNCITY PROVIDENCE—PARKING LOT or
INT. WILSON'S HOUSE—KITCHEN

It's important not to be too vague or ambiguous. For example, "EXT. PROVIDENCE" is brief but not specific or accurate enough. Where in Providence? No need to get too specific here, either. "EXT. RHODE ISLAND—DOWNCITY PROVIDENCE—MAIN STREET—THIRD HOUSE ON THE LEFT" is overkill.

It is also important to specify if the scene takes place during the day or night or somewhere in between. Again, no need to get too specific by writing things like "2 A.M." or "10:30 P.M." Only "DAY," "NIGHT," "DAWN," or "DUSK" are generally used. And we can now add:

EXT. DOWNCITY PROVIDENCE—PARKING LOT—DAY or
INT. WILSON'S HOUSE—KITCHEN—NIGHT

Note that if the audience is supposed to know the exact hour, it must appear elsewhere, like in an image (e.g., subtitled), object (e.g., "the clock reads...."), in stage directions, or in dialogue (e.g., "Hey, don't you know it's already 11:30!"). Other time indicators include:

- CONTINUOUS, which is used when one scene follows the previous one, without any time interruption. (i.e. moving from room to room);

- LATER, which is used when we remain in the same location but we move forward in time (less than day to night); and

- SAME, which can be used to imply that two scenes are happening in different locations at the same time.

Actions or stage directions can be stated once the scene is set. This is when a writer can get creative with everything we see and, other than dialogue, everything we hear. It is important, though, for the writer to be economical with his or her words. Unlike a novel, a script has a finite length, so there's no need to trace every detail of every set piece. Nor should a writer describe every step of every action. Too much irrelevant description will bog down a script.

CHARACTERS

Although a character is not a necessity for each and every scene, at some point one or many will be introduced, either as a speaking role or as someone entering or exiting a scene. So, there are certain rules to introducing characters for the first time. For example, the first time a character physically appears in a scene, his or her name must be capitalized in the stage direction. Following the character's name, some type of description should follow. The description you use depends on the importance of the character and the scene itself. If describing the clothing is important to the scene and the reader's understanding of the character, then it should be included. The same goes for a character's age, hair color, and any other distinguishing characteristics. So, to use one of the scenes we've been working on as an example, character description could be written as:

EXT. DOWNCITY PROVIDENCE—PARKING LOT—DAY
The Parking Lot is vacant except for a few cars on the outskirts. The asphalt is old in appearance and the white lines are barely visible. Lights surround the perimeter. A large building is nearby. BILL, a dark-haired skater-dude in his late teens, is walking and sees TED, a blonde skater-dude also in his late teens.

Note that once a character is introduced using all caps, his or her name should then be written normally throughout the rest of the script.

ADDING SOUNDS AND SIGNS

Similarly, sounds that are not created by a character in the scene need to be capitalized. This is a reminder that although the sound is not in the scene as it is shot, the actors need to account for it during shooting. For example: CHURCH BELLS, KNOCK, EXPLOSION, etc. Also, anything intended for the audience to read must be in caps and placed in quotation marks, such as an "OPEN" sign or a "WELCOME HOME" banner. Let's visit the scene we've been working on again:

EXT. DOWNCITY PROVIDENCE—PARKING LOT—DAY
The Parking Lot is vacant except for a few cars on the outskirts. The asphalt is old in appearance and the white lines are barely visible. Lights surround the perimeter. A large building is nearby. BILL, a

dark-haired skater-dude in his late teens, is walking and sees TED, a blonde skater-dude also in his late teens. THUNDER crashes. There is a sign that reads "CIRCLE K."

CHARACTER CUES

At some point in the script, characters will begin speaking, either as a monologue or as part of a dialogue or larger conversation. For this aspect of scriptwriting, the writer uses **character cues**, which indicate which character is speaking a line of dialogue. There are a few simple rules to keep in mind when working with characters. Say, for instance, that a character's name is Walter Neff. His character is called NEFF in the script, so must remain NEFF throughout the rest of the script. It can't be changed to WALTER later on. If two characters are named John, they both cannot have the cue name JOHN. They should be referred to by their last names—for example, JOHN A. and JOHN Q. For characters that are unnamed, it is common to refer to minor characters by their role, such as POLICEMAN or BARISTA.

DIALOGUE

Dialogue is what a character says. It is the "voice" of a character and everything from the dialogue's content, tone, grammar, rhythm, and accent serve to define the person speaking and establish the character's credibility. Sometimes it is necessary to include other information about the delivery of the dialogue. For example:

- 🎬 Voiceover (V.O.): implies that the person speaking is not speaking from that time and place, like a narrator commenting on the events of a scene.

- 🎬 Off screen (O.S.): implies that the character speaking is present in the time and place of the scene but is not visible from the camera's perspective (i.e., a voice from a phone or from behind a door).

Personal directions refer only to the person speaking the lines within which he or she appears and are usually indicated in parentheses. Personal directions should not be used to tell an actor how to perform his or her lines. The line itself should evoke the emotional tone of the delivery without the script labeling it as such. If a line is not sarcastic, then labeling it with the personal direction "(sarcastically)" will not make it sarcastic. So, when *do* we use personal directions? They are often used for very small actions that must happen during a precise line of dialogue. Note that the character names and all other related text is indented. For example:

KEY TERMS
- **Charcter cues:** in a script, indications of which character is speaking a line of dialogue
- **Dialogue:** the lines spoken by the characters on screen

> BILL
> C'mon Ted, let's be friends.
> (reaches out his hand)
> Let bygones be bygones.

There are times when it may not be clear to whom a character is speaking, so, instead of embedding the name of the character in the lines of dialogue, the writer can simply indicate it in personal directions. For example:

> BILL
> (to Ted)
> C'mon, let's be friends.
> (reaches out his hand)
> Let bygones be bygones.

So, here's what the beginning of our script might look like:

EXT. DOWNCITY PROVIDENCE—PARKING LOT—DAY
The Parking Lot is vacant except for a few cars on the outskirts. The asphalt is old in appearance and the white lines are barely visible. Lights surround the perimeter. A large building is nearby. BILL, a dark haired skater-dude in his late teens, is walking and sees TED, a blonde skater-dude also in his late teens. THUNDER crashes. There is a sign that reads "CIRCLE K."

> BILL
> (to Ted)
> C'mon, let's be friends.
> (reaches out his hand)
> Let bygones be bygones.

That sums up the basic rules of the script writing process. Like a student of the visual arts, equipped with brush and paint and a blank canvas, the student of scriptwriting can begin. After all, a pencil and paper are all that is needed. Like any other discipline, the more students work at the craft and receive feedback, the better writers they will become.

EXERCISE: WRITING A SCRIPT

The following exercise is intended to have the students begin the practice of crafting an individual or group script. The teacher can decide to use this as a starting-off point for a much larger, more involved scriptwriting project or simply use it as an assessment tool for the learning experiences in this chapter. Each of the tasks below correspond to the concepts introduced earlier. The goal, though, is to have the students be creative in their ideas. As long as they adhere to the rules, allow them to be as creative and spontaneous as they wish.

Begin by directing the students to choose a story. It does not have to be an original one, but some students may have stories ready to offer. These ideas may come from a short story they know of, a cartoon they watch, or even a picture book that they enjoy. Young adult novels also work best for some of these introductory lessons. In many cases, the author provides enough written information in the text for the students to adapt into a script (descriptions of setting, character, and dialogue.) Once a story has been settled on, students should then identify the genre it falls into.

Students should then be directed to write a concept, the term that professionals use to describe the main idea of a story. A concept is commonly written as one sentence in the form of a question. Let's look at the concepts for a few popular films written in a question form:

- 🎬 "What if a teenager was able to go back in time to before his parents met?" (*Back to the Future*; Canton, Gale, & Zemeckis, 1985)

- 🎬 "What happens when a gigantic shark begins to attack vacationers on a small island town?" (*Jaws*; Zanuck, Brown, & Spielberg, 1975)

- 🎬 "Can a forgotten young boy become the powerful wizard he was destined to be?" (*Harry Potter and the Sorcerer's Stone*; Heyman & Columbus, 2001)

Note: This exercise can be done over and over again with the class as practice. You could have them write down the titles of five favorite films and the genre and concept next to them.

Now it is time have the students begin to craft a scene. For this they could either draft their work on paper or on a word processing program. There are also many free apps that are set with tabs for character, dialogue, setting, and more. ScriptBuddy is one of my students' favorites. Final Draft is a relatively inexpensive computer program designed with the screenwriter in mind. If one of these is not an option, the students can simply figure out how many tabs or indents to use for their formatting to be correct. They'll get the hang of it. Remind students that they should begin with a scene heading, keeping in mind that the reader will need to know where and when the scene is taking place.

For scene headings, recall that students must decide whether the scene is an interior (INT) or exterior (EXT) scene. Then, they will need to specify where the scene takes place (e.g., A PARKING LOT) and the time of day (e.g., NIGHT or EARLY MORNING). Lastly, they will include a description of the setting. For example:

> The Parking Lot is vacant except for a few cars on the outskirts. The asphalt is old in appearance and the white lines are barely visible. Lights surround the perimeter. A large building is nearby.

Once a setting has been decided upon and written, it is time for students to fill the scene with a character or characters and have them speak in dialogue with each other. This will also include notes on stage direction and action. Try starting them off with a one-page limit, with a possible second-page extension for homework. Students will begin to feel comfortable with the formatting and style that is required when composing a script, and you will be surprised at the excitement and diligence with which they complete the work.

When the introductory assignments are complete, students could be asked to "act" these out in class, or simply to conduct a read-through of the script. There is not any movement during a read-through, only spoken dialogue. Remind the students that they may eventually be crafting their own production in the future and that those with original ideas can continue to work on their scripts on their own time. Some will want to. Let them know you are willing to read their work and to offer suggestions and comments.

FLIPPING THE SCRIPT

Another fun and advanced exercise is one called "Flipping the Script," where students take a short script and "flip" it into a different genre. During this exercise, the students, having been exposed to the elements of genre, will work to adapt parts of a written script into a different genre by changing the story formula, setting, characters, and themes. To do this, simply print out a page or pages from a script and have groups of students utilize the genre posters and chart created during the lessons in the previous chapter. Once they identify the aspects of their script, students can then begin to substitute the story formula, themes, character types, setting, and presentation. There are many resources to share with your students that involve the screenwriting process. Below is a list of some favorites:

BOOKS

- *Screenplay: The Foundations of Screenwriting* by Syd Field (2005)
- *How Not to Write a Screenplay: 101 Common Mistakes Most Screenwriters Make* by Denny Martin Flinn (1999)
- *Lew Hunter's Screenwriting 434: The Industry's Premier Teacher Reveals the Secrets of the Successful Screenplay* by Lew Hunter (2004)
- *The 101 Habits Of Highly Successful Screenwriters: Insider Secrets from Hollywood's Top Writers* by Karl Iglesias (2011)
- *The Screenwriter's Bible: A Complete Guide to Writing, Formatting, and Selling Your Script* (6th ed.) by David Trottier (2014)

WEBSITES

- Screenwriters Utopia: http://www.screenwritersutopia.com
- Information on copyrighting a script: http://www.copyright.gov/

CHAPTER 5

CINEMATOGRAPHY
THE CAMERA IS YOUR EYE IS THE CAMERA

Once a script is complete—meaning it has been revised and edited—preparations for filming can begin. The scripts are passed around to all of the folks responsible for bringing the script to life on the screen. Costumes are made, sets are built based on an artist's rendering, casting for actors begins, and the myriad tasks described in Chapter 1 can begin, ultimately creating the mise-en-scène that will be filmed. Although it is the director who has control over what's in front of the camera, it's the cinematographer, or more commonly known as the director of photography (DP), who is in charge of how to capture scenes through the lens. It is now time to introduce your students to the world of cinematography.

It is important at this point to stress to the students that they should start thinking about the camera itself as a substitute for the eye, and not only their own, but the audience's too. There are many ways to accomplish what the DP wants the audience to view on the screen. The DP's pockets are full of a variety of techniques at his or her disposal.

In everyday life, there is an attachment formed with things close to us. So too is our connection to what we see on the screen. Moods can be created with the position of the camera. For example, a character onscreen in what is called a "**close-up**" will generate much more sympathy (if that's the desired effect) from the viewer than a

KEY TERM

- **Close-up:** a camera shot that frames the subject filling nearly the entire screen; framing of the human figure from the neck up

KEY TERM

• **Long shot:** a camera shot that shows an object as small with the background dominating; framing the human figure from head to toe

character framed in a "**long shot**." If the mood is to feel spooky, then certain filters and exposures can accomplish this. If the camera tilts to the side or shakes violently, the audience feels it too, and it is often uncomfortable. In this era of Instagram, Snapchat, and other smartphone apps, be assured that your students will easily understand many of the techniques that will be covered in the following sections. We've also provided some examples of storyboard illustration to depict specific camera shots and angles. Once introduced, you, and eventually your students, will begin to recognize them in films watched. Remember to use whatever examples work for you.

HOW THE SHOT LOOKS

There are a few ways to change the very nature of what is being captured on film. The first involves film stock. Film stock refers to the unexposed film used for recording movies. In the early days of film, a filmmaker had many choices when it came to film stock, but in the early 1900s, 35-millimeter (35-mm) film became the standard gauge. Manufacturers also made 8-mm and 16-mm film, which became popular not only for amateurs but also independent filmmakers who were attracted to less expensive stocks. An added benefit was the "look" achieved, as images appeared darker and grainier onscreen.

Choosing the frame rate (i.e., how many frames are recorded per second) also alters the look of the film. Without getting too involved in the science of film, a certain amount of images must be displayed through a projector within each second to give the appearance of movement. In the early days of cinema, films were shot and projected at 16 frames per second (fps), a seemingly fine speed at which to project film. However, if you go back and look at these films, you'll notice a flicker on screen, along with sped-up action. This led to these films being called flicks, a term we still use today. When sound was introduced to cinema in 1926, the standard became 24 fps, and that standard stuck until digital film was introduced. Because of the advanced picture quality with digital film, it is necessary to film and project at a larger fps, in most cases 29.97 or 30.

Digital cameras and camcorders allow for many effects that mimic the choices filmmakers had when they had only film to record on. There are even apps that turn your device's camera into a 16-mm or 8-mm camera, recording in the style of that time, complete with built-in scratches and frame shifts. The effect is quite realistic. Filmmakers can also change the look of their film with the use of lens filters, which change what type of light enters into the lens of the camera. Just like film stock, filters can be manually installed on the lens of a camera (similar to sunglasses or colored light screens) or may be an added effect through a digital medium. It is recommended that you take a look at the following clips in order to compare the graphic qualities of each film:

🎬 The final scene from *O Brother, Where Art Thou?* (Coen & Coen, 2000): https://www.youtube.com/watch?v=OouuZzqaQbU

🎬 The "Do You Steal" clip from Wes Anderson's *Moonrise Kingdom* (Rudin, Rales, Dawson, & Anderson, 2012): https://www.youtube.com/watch?v=2OOenYz6tfc

🎬 The opening sequence from *Double Indemnity* (DeSylva, Sistrom, & Wilder, 1944): https://www.youtube.com/watch?v=EcjfAAOBQx0

Share what you find with your students or simply screen them and have them discuss the nature of each and how they affect the "feel" of the film.

HOW LONG IS THE SHOT ONSCREEN?

All shots have a measurable length. Shots that are onscreen for a longer amount of time should tell the audience a lot. A **take** is one uninterrupted run of the camera. A **long take** gives the audience time to scan the screen and pick up on cues. Why focus on that dog for so long? Well, because in a few scenes, he will become important. Why did we just travel through an office window, down the corridor, around the corner, up the stairs, and come out on the street running, all in one shot? It is all about the effect and how it will tell the story and appeal to the audience. Likewise, a short take is meant to be short. The use of long and short takes creates a pace and rhythm onscreen.

A good example of a film that uses long takes is Hitchcock's *Rope* (Bernstein & Hitchcock, 1948). Hitchcock tried to shoot the entire film without any noticeable cuts. The result is a series of long takes and sequence shots with hidden edits. Another example is the opening of Orson Welles's (1958) *Touch of Evil*. Here, a much more elaborate example of a long take uses crowds of actors, crane shots, and multiple plot lines. To show how short takes can effect a scene, refer to the cancan scene from *Moulin Rouge!* (Baron, Brown, & Luhrmann, 2001). Here, the viewer is treated to a frenzied dance number that creates a dizzying rhythm. Clips from each film can be found on YouTube.

KEY TERMS
- **Take:** one uninterrupted run of the camera
- **Long take:** a shot that continues for an unusually lengthy time before transitioning to the next shot

KEY TERM
• **Framing:** using the edges of the frame to select what will be seen on screen

WHAT IS BEING CAPTURED?

When a picture is taken, everything that appears in the viewfinder or on your digital screen is preserved within the confines of that space. Film is a series of still images, filled with characters and camera movement. This concept of creating space is called **framing** and there are many elements to consider when composing a frame of film. Explain to your students that each shot should be as thoughtful as if it were a classic painting. Alright, maybe not *that* thoughtful, but the act of stopping a film at any moment should result in a meaningful still frame filled with information. Framing goes hand in hand with the following items.

BALANCE

Filmmakers try as best as they can to create balance in each frame. As viewers, the audience is comfortable with order. Obviously, the balancing of shots is a matter of mise-en-scène as much as it is of cinematography. Thus, the placement of objects in the frame (the element of mise-en-scène referred to as *staging*) is crucial in the creation of balance. It is the cinematographer who chooses how to frame the mise-en-scène. Figure 5.1 is a sketch depicting balanced framing, while Figure 5.2 illustrates unbalanced framing.

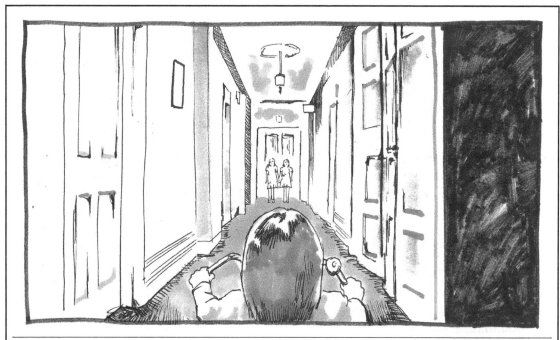

FIGURE 5.1. THIS SHOT FROM STANLEY KUBRICK'S (1980) *THE SHINING* ILLUSTRATES A PERFECTLY BALANCED FRAMING.

FIGURE 5.2. THIS SHOT FROM RIDLEY SCOTT'S *BLADE RUNNER* (DEELEY & SCOTT, 1982) IS AN EXAMPLE OF AN UNBALANCED SHOT. THE SUBJECT, THE CHARACTER ON THE RIGHT, IS THE MAIN FOCUS WITH A GREAT DEAL OF EMPTY SPACE ON THE LEFT. THE EXPECTATION IS THAT SOMETHING OR SOMEONE WILL ENTER THE FRAME FROM THE LEFT TO RESTORE THE BALANCE OF THE SHOT.

FOCUS

The cinematographer chooses what is in focus at any given point, thereby directing the audience's attention to different elements onscreen. **Selective focus** involves the cinematographer setting up a shot and choosing which areas of the screen are in focus; the foreground, middle ground, or background. **Racking or pulling focus** involves changing what is in focus while the camera is running. This is often seen during conversations, when the cinematographer will shift focus between who is speaking.

A great way to illustrate this for students is to direct them in a short activity. Begin by having all of the students except two line up against the front wall of the classroom. Place the remaining two at desks, one in the front of the room and one in the back. Have each student at the front of the room focus with their eyes on the seated student closest to them; they should begin to notice that the student in the back is out of focus in their peripheral vision. Then have the students switch focus to the student in the back of the class and discuss the results. This is also a great way to reinforce

FIGURE 5.3. A SHOT FROM CHRISTOPHER NOLAN'S *THE DARK KNIGHT* DEPICTS THE COMMON USE OF SELECTIVE FOCUS. BRUCE WAYNE IS IN SHARP FOCUS WHILE THE BACKGROUND IS BLURRY.

KEY TERMS

- **Deep focus:** using the camera lens and lighting to keep objects in both close and distant planes in focus
- **Straight-on angle:** the framing of a shot where there is no angle, just a natural straight ahead view of the subject
- **High angle:** a shot where the camera is placed above the subject, looking down

the "camera as the eye" concept, because the camera lens works in much the same way as the eye.

Deep focus is a bit more complicated. Many filmmakers opt not to choose what's in focus for the audience; instead, they use the technique of deep focus to create a shot in which all of the planes (the "grounds") are in focus at the same time. This way, the audience gets to decide what they wish to focus on. In the early 1940s, filmmakers Orson Welles and William Wyler began to perfect this technique, filming entire scenes in one take, the camera remaining motionless, allowing the audience to choose what to focus on. Figure 5.3 through 5.5 depict examples of different types of focus.

CAMERA ANGLE

When it comes to framing, the cinematographer has countless choices to make with regard to where the camera will be when it records. This involves decisions about the angle, level, height, and distance of the camera, all of which have the capability to alter the meaning of any given shot.

Of course, the number of angles one could use is huge, because the camera can be placed almost anywhere. In the world of cinema, there is typically a distinction between three general angle categories. The **straight-on angle** offers a view that is straight in line with the frame. Think of the camera as being placed at the eye level. The audience is present among the actors. The **high angle**, positioned to look down, can be used to accomplish a variety of effects. A character might need to look inferior or weak, or a man on a ledge

FIGURE 5.4. THIS SHOT FROM PETER LORD AND NICK PARK'S *CHICKEN RUN* SHOWS HOW RACKING FOCUS WORKS. IN THE TOP CLIP THE CHICKEN IS IN CLEAR FOCUS WITH THE BACKGROUND OUT OF FOCUS. THE BOTTOM CLIP SWITCHES ITS FOCUS TO THE CHARACTER IN THE BACKGROUND, LEAVING THE CHICKEN BLURRY. THIS OCCURS WHILE THE CAMERA STILL RUNNING.

FIGURE 5.5. THE SHOT FROM ORSON WELLES'S (1941) *CITIZEN KANE* SHOWS HIS USE OF DEEP FOCUS. HERE ALL THE PLANES (FOREGROUND, MIDDLE GROUND, AND BACKGROUND) ARE IN SHARP FOCUS, ALLOWING THE AUDIENCE TO CHOOSE WHAT TO FOCUS ON.

might have a perilous view. The **low angle**, positioned to look up, can also convey a variety of feelings. This angle's main function is to make a character or subject look superior, powerful, and imposing, but it can also be used to show the point of view of a character who is hiding. Figures 5.6 and 5.7 show examples of a high angle and a low angle.

FIGURE 5.6. THIS SHOT FROM BAZ LUHRMMAN'S *MOULIN ROUGE!* (BARON, BROWN, & LUHRMANN, 2001) COMES AT A VERY WEAK MOMENT FOR THE CHARACTER. HIS LOVE HAS DIED, SO A HIGH ANGLE SHOT IS USED TO SHOW HIS STATE OF MIND.

FIGURE 5.7. A SHOT FROM TIM BURTON'S *EDWARD SCISSORHANDS* (DI NOVI & BURTON, 1990) GIVES AN EXAMPLE OF A LOW ANGLE SHOT. AT THIS MOMENT, EDWARD HAS STARTED TO BE ACCEPTED BY A PART OF THE COMMUNITY.

LEVEL

Most, if not all, of the shots in any given film will be level. However, sometimes the cinematographer may tilt the frame to one side to create a skewed view of a scene. These shots are typical in the horror and film noir genres. The industry terms for tipping a frame to one side are **Dutch angle** or **canted angle**. Figure 5.8 is an example of a canted angle.

KEY TERM
• Dutch angle: a framing of a shot that is not level; also called a canted angle

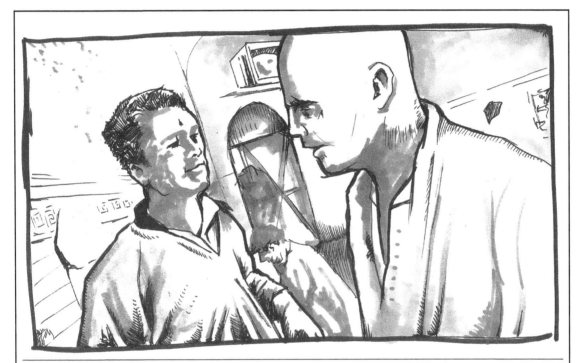

FIGURE 5.8. THIS SHOT FROM TERRY GILLIAM'S *12 MONKEYS* SHOWS AN EXAMPLE OF A DUTCH ANGLE. IN A MENTAL HOSPITAL, THE MAIN CHARACTER IS DEALING IN A CONFUSING, OFF-KILTER UNIVERSE. THE DUTCH ANGLE HELPS EXPRESS HIS MENTAL AND EMOTIONAL STATE TO THE AUDIENCE.

HEIGHT

The camera is always positioned at a certain height as well. Height is different from angle because the view remains straight on no matter what height the camera is placed at. For the most part, the camera is placed at the height of an average person, looking straight on. This is not always the case. In François Truffaut's *The 400 Blows* (Charlot & Truffaut, 1959), the camera is almost always shooting from Antoine's perspective. Meaning, the camera is actually placed at the height of a child, most of the time looking up onto the scene. But the camera also usually stays on Antoine, revealing his reactions, making the audience feel what he feels and see what he sees. Figure 5.9 is an example of camera height.

FIGURE 5.9. THE SCENE FROM *THE 400 BLOWS* (CHARLOT & TRUFFAUT, 1959) IN WHICH ANTIONE RETURNS THE STOLEN TYPEWRITER IS PRIMARILY SHOT FROM HIS (A CHILD'S) HEIGHT. WHEN THE ADULT ENTERS THE FRAME, HE MUST BE SEATED FOR THE AUDIENCE TO SEE HIS EXPRESSION.

KEY TERMS

- **Extreme long shot:** a camera shot in which the landscape or background dominates; the human figure is barely visible
- **Long shot:** a camera shot that shows an object as small with the background dominating; framing the human figure from head to toe
- **Medium long shot:** a camera shot which shows the majority of an object with the background still visible; framing the human figure from about the knees up
- **Medium shot:** a camera shot which shows an object in moderate size in the frame; framing the human figure from about the waist up

Continues on page 55

DISTANCE

In matters of framing, all images are seen at some distance. Filmmakers typically use the human body's visibility as a measure for camera distances. Each of the following "shots" present the variety of ways a human body may be filmed.

In the **extreme long shot**, the human figure is barely visible. This is the framing used for landscapes and bird's-eye views. The **long shot** presents the human figure as more prominent, but the background still dominates the frame. We still are able to see the body from head to toe. A **medium long shot** captures the human figure framed from about the knees up and a **medium shot** frames the human body from the waist up. There is the **medium close-up,** which frames the body from chest up, and the **close-up**, traditionally a shot showing just the head, hands, or feet. It is meant to emphasize facial expressions, the details of a gesture, or a significant object. Finally, the **extreme close-up** singles out a portion of the face, often the eyes, or isolates and magnifies an object. Figures 5.10 through 5.15 are examples of everything from an extreme long shot to an extreme close-up.

FIGURE 5.10. IN AN EXTREME LONG SHOT (ELS OR XLS), THE HUMAN FIGURE IS BARELY VISIBLE. THIS FRAMING IS COMMONLY USED FOR LANDSCAPES AND BIRDS-EYE VIEWS.

Continued from page 54

- **Medium close-up:** a camera shot which shows an object fairly large in the frame; framing the human figure from about the chest up
- **Close-up:** a camera shot that frames the subject filling nearly the entire screen; framing of the human figure from the neck up
- **Extreme close-up:** a camera shot in which an object fills the frame, most commonly a small object or part of the body

FIGURE 5.11. A LONG SHOT (LS) FEATURES THE HUMAN FIGURE PROMINENTLY, BUT THE BACKGROUND STILL DOMINATES THE FRAME. THE BODY IS VISIBLE FROM HEAD TO TOE.

FIGURE 5.12. A MEDIUM LONG SHOT (MLS; ALSO CALLED THE AMERICAN SHOT) FRAMES THE HUMAN FIGURE FROM ABOUT THE KNEES UP.

FIGURE 5.13. A MEDIUM SHOT (MS) FRAMES THE HUMAN BODY FROM THE WAIST UP.

FIGURE 5.14. A MEDIUM CLOSE-UP (MCU) FRAMES THE BODY FROM THE CHEST UP.

FIGURE 5.15. A CLOSE-UP (CU) SHOWS JUST THE HEAD, HANDS, OR FEET. IT EMPHASIZES FACIAL EXPRESSIONS, THE DETAILS OF A GESTURE, OR A SIGNIFICANT OBJECT.

CAMERA MOVEMENT

Before we wrap this chapter, it is important to point out that the frame does have the ability to move. **Mobile framing**, as it's called, means that the framing of the object changes the camera angle, level, height, and distance *during* the shot. We usually refer to the ability of the frame to move as camera movement, and there are several kinds of camera movement, each having a specific effect onscreen.

A **tilt shot** rotates the camera up and down, as if the camera's head were nodding "yes." The **pan shot** (short for panorama) has a movement that rotates the camera side to side (head turning left and right.) On screen, the pan gives the impression of horizontally scanning the area, as if the camera turns its head right or left. Try these movements with your students.

A **tracking shot** is one where the camera moves parallel to the ground. That can mean forward, backward, circularly, diagonally, or from side to side. There are a few different techniques to tracking:

🎬 A dolly shot means the camera is attached to a dolly or any platform with wheels. This technique is used to follow actors walking in the street, etc.

KEY TERMS
- **Mobile framing:** also referred to as camera movement; the change of framing during a shot
- **Tilt shot:** a camera movement on a stationary axis that moves up and down
- **Pan shot:** a camera movement on a stationary axis from right to left or left to right
- **Tracking shot:** a type of camera movement that follows a subject's movement

- A trucking shot requires the mounting of a camera on a flatbed truck. Filmmakers will use this type of tracking to shoot car chases.

- A steadicam mounts the camera to the operator with a harness. This might be used to follow a character running through the woods. Because it is mounted with a harness, the steadicam limits any shaky, jolted movement.

- A hand-held shot is when the operator holds the camera. This usually results in very shaky action on screen.

- A crane shot is when the camera moves above ground level. Typically, it rises or descends, often due to a mechanical arm that lifts and lowers the camera. Think of a camera on a cherry picker. Figure 5.16 is an example of a crane shot from Hitchcock's (1946) *Notorious*. Note the camera shadow on the right side of the image. The use of the crane allowed Hitchcock to go from a panning long shot of a party to an extreme close-up of an actress' hand (see figure 5.17).

FIGURE 5.16. LONG SHOT EXAMPLE FROM THE DIRECTOR'S PERSPECTIVE ON THE CRANE.

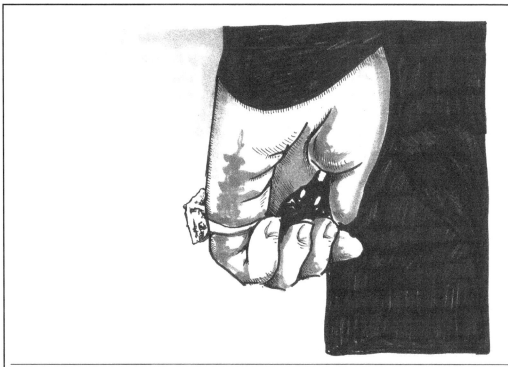

FIGURE 5.17. CLOSE-UP SHOT OF THE SAME SETTING WITH A FOCUS ON AN OBJECT, ALSO SHOT FROM THE CRANE.

HANDS-ON CINEMATOGRAPHY WORKSHOP

A great culmination to this lesson on cinematography involves a creative assignment that introduces the students to the use of a camera and has them begin to learn to "shoot." Start with a short introduction to the workings of the camera. This includes focusing (no pun intended) on zooming in and out, how to capture an image or video clip, and how to attach the camera to a tripod, if they choose to incorporate one while completing the assignment. Some of your students will possess an expert knowledge in using a camera and some will require assistance. The use of smart devices can also be presented as an option.

This assignment can be completed individually or in groups. The objective is for the students to shoot the alphabet from A to Z, in any way possible. The only rule is that they must include all of the 13 shots in the checklist provided in Handout 5.1 at least once. Other than that, they can interpret the assignment in any way they choose. Final products can be shown in class. The goal is not to make a film, but simply to have the students utilize each of the major shot types now at their disposal.

Like in many of the chapters in this book, it may be necessary to screen an entire film or parts of a film to further illustrate the technique being discussed. The study guide below is designed for a screening of the Stephen Spielberg classic, *Jaws* (Zanuck, Brown, & Spielberg, 1975), but it can easily be adapted for use with a different film example. The questions within the study guide can be assigned as homework or in-class work after the film has finished. It will certainly aid in class discussions about film and cinematography. Other suggested screenings include:

- Beginner: *Moonrise Kingdom* (Rudin, Rales, Dawson, & Anderson, 2012)
- Intermediate: *Notorious* (Hitchcock, 1946)
- Advanced: *The 400 Blows* (Charlot & Truffaut, 1959)

STUDY GUIDE
JAWS

1. When thinking about cinematography we must ask firstly, "*Where is the camera?*" The choices a cinematographer makes about camera placement have a direct effect on the audience's experience. Give three examples of the framing of the images in *Jaws*—how does it influence our experience of the film?

2. In what ways do filmmakers "manipulate" their audiences? Why do you feel certain emotions when watching a film (such as empathy, anxiety, etc.)? How were you "directed" when watching *Jaws*?

3. Mobile framing is defined as the framing of an object that changes the camera angle, level, height, and distance *during* the shot. What are some examples of camera movement in *Jaws*? What is the effect of these moving camera shots?

Name: _____ Date: _____

SHOT CHECKLIST

	Shot Complete	**Letter Used**
Extreme Long Shot		
Long Shot		
Medium Long Shot		
Medium Shot		
Medium Close-Up		
Close-Up		
Extreme Close-Up		
Low Angle		
High Angle		
Pan—Right		
Pan—Left		
Tilt—Up		
Tilt—Down		

CHAPTER 6

PARTS TO A WHOLE

EDITING

Introducing the concept and process of editing can present a few hiccups as you work to decide which program to use and how to teach it. Many of the available editing programs are designed in a way that both beginners and professionals can use them with ease. Tutorials, provided by the manufacturer or a trusted online help site, can help the students quickly understand the inner workings of a particular program. Honestly, and again we feel like we have said this over and over again, many of your students will have first-hand experience with a particular program, and can provide assistance and tutoring to those who don't. Planning to teach the vastness of some of the bigger programs like FinalCut Pro or Adobe Premiere Pro might require an entire semester or even a full-year course. Rest assured, there is enough power in the stripped-down versions to get them started.

Depending on your school budget, you will have to settle for what you can afford. Don't despair—there are basic and free programs available to you, like iMovie for Macs and Windows Movie Maker for Windows-based systems, provided that you have access to a PC/laptop or an Apple computer. You can also purchase FinalCut Elements or Adobe Premier, which are less hefty versions of the popular programs, and run at around $100. There are also a few good free or pay-per-space programs available as apps in the Google world.

KEY TERMS

- **Editing:** selecting and putting footage together
- **Cut (or straight cut):** the joining of two shots together without space or overlap
- **Fade:** (1) fade-in: a black screen that gradually brightens as the shot appears; (2) fade-out: a shot that gradually disappears as the screen darkens
- **Dissolve:** a transition between two shots during which the first shot is briefly superimposed over the second shot
- **Wipe:** a transition between two shots during which a line crosses the screen, eliminating one shot and replacing it with the next

WeVideo, a cloud-based program, provides what you will need to introduce the concept of editing.

It is important to find a balance between a lecture-style tutorial and hands-on training for your students. Although it is sometimes necessary for you to be in front of the classroom, navigating and clicking through the program as your students sit and watch, more crucial is the time when you can assist as they work through their own material. Try to teach a small aspect of the process and then have the students apply what you have taught them. This may be in the form of a hands-on workshop where students can utilize their work from the alphabet assignment in Chapter 5. You may also ask the students to bring in photos and video clips from their own personal collections. Remember that the goal is for them to learn technique and terminology. Cinematic masterpieces are not the end result . . . yet.

Now, let us look at **editing**, the process filmmakers use to put their footage together. Editing is a complicated process and involves much more than placing clips together in a particular order. As you will find out later in the chapter, the editing process requires a good deal of thinking on the part of the editor. The ways in which camera angles and framing are utilized are considered an art, as each individual director/editor combination creates something new. Editing also involves the addition of special effects, the enhancement of sound, and the correction of color. Just think, a feature-length film contains between 1,000 to 2,000 shots, meaning that between those shots exist the same amount of edits.

There are four common ways to join shots as part of the same scene. The most used edit is the **cut**, or straight cut. Here, two shots are spliced together end to end with no overlap or space in between. If a shot fades to black, it's called **fade-out**, and if a shot fades in from black, it's called **fade-in**. A **dissolve** briefly superimposes the end of the first shot over the beginning of the second, and in a **wipe**, the second shot replaces the first as a frame line moves across the screen. Like a dissolve, both images are on screen at the same time, but they do not overlap, in fact they appear to be pushed aside.

When editing, it is important that the scenes created from shots feel continuous and uninterrupted, regardless of what technique is used. It is of the utmost importance that the two shots next to each other make sense, both narratively and visually. Therefore, an editor must make choices about how putting shots together forces the audience to make visual connections. Editors create a rhythm and imply relations based on space.

When two shots are edited together, the editor must also decide how the color, lighting, and overall tone of a scene compare. If the film is shot in sepia tones, for instance, followed by a shot in Technicolor, it may disorient the viewer. In a nutshell, shots must remain consistent within each scene.

Exploring deeper, a filmmaker may link shots by graphic similarities, creating what's called a **graphic match**. This occurs when shapes, colors, or the overall composition or movement found in Shot A are in sync with the composition of Shot B (Shots within scenes are often labeled with letter). Take the scene in Spielberg's *Jaws* (Zanuck, Brown, & Spielberg, 1975), directly after the little boy, Alex, is killed. The shot of his mother's yellow hat is matched with Alex's deflated raft in color and texture. This clip can be found at the end of the YouTube video found at https://www.youtube.com/watch?v=_2Ecwm7Alrc, and the shots are represented in Figure 6.1.

KEY TERM
- **Graphic match:** two shots joined together to create a similarity of visual elements (e.g., color, shape, etc.)

FIGURE 6.1. BOTH THE RAFT AND THE WOMAN'S HAT ARE YELLOW, RESULTING IN A GRAPHIC MATCH BETWEEN THE TWO SHOTS.

KEY TERM
- Parallel editing: also referred to as crosscutting, editing that alternates between two or more events occurring in different places

An editor must also decide how long to keep each shot onscreen. In doing this, the editor creates a rhythm by placing shots of varying or similar length together. He or she may choose a series of short takes put together intended to speed up the pace or give the audience an anxious feeling. A series of long takes are intended to draw out the action, slowing it down and offering moments for reflection and drama. Most editors use a combination of long and short takes, but it is crucial that an editor create a pace to the film through editing, successfully accomplished by paying attention to the length of each shot and the combination of shots in a scene. Keep in mind that cinematic rhythm doesn't come directly from the editing of shots alone. Movement in the mise-en-scène, camera position, sound, and the overall context of the script all aid in the editing rhythm too.

So, editing any two shots together implies that they are related in some way, but the power of editing also allows the audience to relate these two spaces on many more levels. In other words, film editors can create spaces and distances that don't already exist. The audience can travel from the classroom to Mars in one easy cut. Have your students think about it like this:

If we were to film one shot of you walking out the door from inside the classroom, then cut to a shot of you walking out of a spaceship, it will seem like this room is the inside of that spaceship, right? That's the power of editing. By simply putting two shots next to each other, we can imply that the spaces in each shot are related, even if they are not on the same planet!

Editing can also emphasize action that takes place in separate locations. **Parallel editing**, or crosscutting, is when two spaces are edited together to suggest two events are happening simultaneously. Many films use crosscutting to show two separate actions that are meant to be perceived as happening simultaneously. Hitchcock's (1951) *Strangers on a Train*, particularly the scenes in which Bruno and Guy are racing to the carnival, illustrates a perfect example of this. You can access the scenes at http://www.youtube.com/watch?v=KPLZAH987J4.

THE KULESHOV EFFECT

Lev Kuleshov was a filmmaker who lived in the Soviet Union during the 1920s. He is probably most known for a series of film experiments he conducted during that time. In his most famous one, Kuleshov cut a shot of an actor's expressionless face with shots of soup, nature scenes, a dead woman, and a baby. The audience would see a shot of the actor and then a shot of soup, then the same unchanged shot of the actor, then a nature scene, and so on. After a screening, the audience immediately assumed that the actor's expression changed with each new cut in reaction to the images and that they were present in the same space. In fact, the images had nothing to do with each other.

This came to be known as the **Kuleshov Effect,** and the effect works because of the absence of an **establishing shot,** one that usually involves a distant framing that shows the spatial relations among the important figures, objects, and setting in a scene. Simply put, a long shot of a classroom will allow the audience to see everything in it, therefore establishing that it is a classroom with tables, chairs, and students. Once the setting is established, the editor can then switch to closer shots of the action. The audience will maintain that the action takes place in a classroom.

The Kuleshov Effect takes away this establishing shot, making the audience assume that all the actions they are seeing are taking place in the same space. The soup and the man were never shown together, so the audience assumes that they are because the shots followed one another. There is a great example of this, along with some great insight into editing and the film *Psycho* (Hitchcock, 1960), in an interview titled, "Fletcher Markle: A Talk With Hitchcock," which can be found on YouTube: https://www.youtube.com/watch?v=xkpxFWVoKw8.

A WORD OR TWO ABOUT TIME

The unique function of editing also gives the editor the ability to manipulate time. An editor may alter the order of events, the duration of a specific event, and may increase or decrease the frequency of when we see an event.

The editor, under direction from the director, chooses the order in which we will see the events unfold on screen. Some films depict events in chronological order—the order in which they actually occur in time. It is a "lived" experience for the audience. One thing happens, then the next thing, then the next. There are times however, when an editor opts to show the narrative events out of order. The most common example is referred to as a **flashback,** when an event that has happened previously in the character's life (onscreen or inferred) is shown during a present event. Thus, flashbacks help fill in backstory, trigger memory, and so on.

A much rarer option for reordering story events is the **flash-forward.** Unlike flashbacks that move from the present to the past and then back again, flash-forward moves from the present to some future event and then returns to the present. This type of time manipulation is most common in science fiction films. There are also instances when a film depicts a character's vision of the future, even though these visions are not actual events but merely suppositions of a possible future.

During a film we do not need to see every single event of a character's life. That would be quite boring. A film need only show major events that are important to the overall arc of the story. Therefore, through editing, the filmmaker will often leave unimportant details out. This is called **elliptical editing.** Here, the audience sees some action onscreen in less time than it might actually take in the story. For example, if a film shows the beginning of some action, like climbing the stairs, but then cuts and dissolves to a shot of the end of that action, reaching the top of the staircase, the audience will still understand that the stairs were climbed without having to see the entire process, right?

An editor can also insert a shot of some other event, happening in some other place, between actions. This is called a **cutaway.** Let us use the same staircase example. The editor can cut from the first shot of a man climbing the stairs to a shot of a man standing in an upstairs room, then back to the man reaching the top of the stairs. The cutaway shot of the man in the room takes away the need to watch the entire ascension, while also giving the audience new information.

Sometimes it is necessary to show a large-scale process or a lengthy period in a short amount of time. This is where a **montage sequence** is used. By joining images with dissolves and music, filmmakers can compress a lengthy series of action into a few moments. These types of sequencing are popular in sports movies like the Rocky series, but are not limited to that genre. Trey Parker's *Team America: World Police* (Rudin, Stone, & Parker, 2004) has a great example as well with the montage about montages featuring a song called "Montage." The Pixar animation *Up* (Rivera & Docter, 2009) also shows the power of montage in the opening sequence as we see the main character Carl's life in a matter of minutes. The webzine Total Film has a great list of the "50 Greatest Movie Montages": http://www.totalfilm. com/features/50-greatest-movie-montages.

CONTINUITY

It is very important for film editors to maintain **continuity** throughout the film while creating a smooth flow from shot to shot. This is because good editing should go unnoticed. The point is for the shots and images to appear seamless to the audience. There are four ways an editor can build and maintain continuity:

1. The composition of the image (how it looks) is usually kept consistent from shot to shot.
2. Figures in the frame are usually balanced and the action is centered in the frame.
3. The lighting is kept consistent and relates to the mood.
4. The film utilizes the 180-degree system (see explanation below).

The **180-degree system** is the most important tool for young filmmakers as they go out on location to shoot their films and is crucial for maintaining continuity. If we think about the possible area to be filmed as a circle, there is an invisible line that bisects the circle. Knowing and visualizing this, the filmmaker may shoot from any point on the correct side of the line. This line is referred to as the axis of action, center line, or 180-degree line. The dotted line in Figure 6.2 models the axis of action. The cameras below are placed in a way that establishes and sustains the line. The camera can be placed anywhere as long as it stays on the same side. To cut to a shot from the camera above (Camera X), or to any point on the other side of the line, would violate the system because it crosses the axis of action and will confuse the audience. The 180-degree system helps to keep the following consistent:

- Character's eyelines: A character looking left should be consistently looking that way. If the line is crossed, the left looking character will then be looking right.

- Where a character is: A character standing on the right side of the frame should remain on the right. Shooting from the opposite side of the line will switch the positions and be quite disorienting.

- Screen direction: Filming from the correct side of the line will maintain a character's direction as he or she walks left to right across the line. Switching to a camera on the opposite side will make the character appear to be switching directions.

There are many ways to have your students experiment with the process of editing. The best way to ensure understanding is to provide a quick tutorial of a program, highlight what to use, and let them play for as long as they want. The more they explore, the more they will uncover and become familiar with.

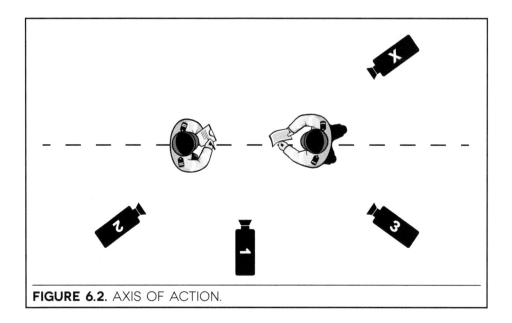

FIGURE 6.2. AXIS OF ACTION.

KEY TERMS
- **Ingesting:** in digital editing, the act of importing footage into a computer
- **Timeline:** in nonlinear editing, the timeline is an interface that enables editors to lay a video project out in a linear fashion horizontally across a monitor

AN EXERCISE: RE-EDITING A COMMERCIAL

Begin by having the students access downloadable clips found at the following website: http://www.routledge.com/cw/butler-9780415883283/s1/ video/. Along with the clips, you will find complete directions and an explanation of the editing exercise. It is worth the time.

This exercise allows beginner filmmakers to work with footage that has already been shot. Therefore, they can work on importing footage into an editing program (also called "**ingesting**") without worrying about things that many young filmmakers are challenged with (e.g., which shots to choose, sound issues, etc.) Students are also exposed to the skill of categorizing and sorting footage, working with clips in the **timeline**, and basic edits.

With projects such as this, I find it works better to give little to no limitations. Let the students edit the footage in any way they choose. The end result does not have to be a car commercial! In fact, it shouldn't be a car commercial. A word of advice when using this exercise: The user can also download the commercial in its entirety as it was intended to be edited. Hold off on showing your students the original so as not to put ideas into their heads.

Aspiring editors will also find this exercise helpful, because it is the editors who are given footage that they didn't shoot and it is up to them to put the clips into some sort of decipherable narrative. Of course, they will have a script to work from (and a director over their shoulder), but this exercise will ultimately illustrate how different the end result can be when put into the hands of multiple filmmakers and editors.

As mentioned earlier, screening of an entire film or scenes will help illustrate the technique being discussed. The study guide below is designed for a screening of Hitchcock's (1960) *Psycho*. Other suggested screenings include:

- Beginner: *Star Wars: A New Hope* (Kurtz & Lucas, 1977)
- Intermediate: *Citizen Kane* (Welles, 1941)
- Advanced: *Run Lola Run** (Arndt & Tykwer, 1998)

STUDY GUIDE
PSYCHO

1. The concept of continuity editing is to allow space, time, and action to continue in a smooth flow over a series of shots. What noticeable techniques, if any, did Hitchcock use in *Psycho* to ensure narrative continuity? Any examples of crosscutting, the use of establishing shots, shot/reverse shot, match on action, etc.? To what effect did he use these techniques?

2. The shower sequence is one of the most famous in the history of cinema. Hitchcock used a variety of techniques in editing, music, and camera angles to disturb the audience and suggest terrible violence and bloodshed without actually showing very much. How does not showing the violence add to the horror? How is this sequence effective, rhythmically and/or graphically?

3. The transitions between scenes in this film are interesting. Our understanding is that transitions refer to a passage of time. Describe some of the scene transitions in *Psycho*. How do they function to cue the audience in reference to time?

4. The opening credits have horizontal and vertical lines repeated in different patterns. Do you see these strong vertical and horizontal "lines" repeated elsewhere in the film? Why might these horizontal and vertical lines (and boxes) be significant? What might they represent?

SOUND

WATCHING WITH YOUR EARS

In the early days of cinema, the technology of film did not allow for the recording of sound. As a result, the theater-going experience for audiences at this time was quite different than it is now. It wasn't until 1926 that the ability to record sound for film was invented. Even though there existed no recorded dialogue before this time, movies were rarely viewed in complete silence. Movies were typically accompanied by an orchestra, organist, or some other music, and dialogue was presented as filmed text in between scenes.

At the onset of this chapter it must be said that silence, unless intentional, is never present in a film. The score (instrumental music), soundtrack (recorded song), dialogue (characters speaking), or sound effects (added extras) fill the void created from the images the audience views on screen. What is heard is created separately from the images and so it, too, can be altered and edited separately. Sound can provide very strong effects, and if done well, has the ability to go unnoticed. So, in order to study sound, we must learn to listen to films, not just view them.

Music is a very powerful tool, often directing the audience how to feel, react, or what to expect. As our example above proves, simply changing the song associated with a scene changes the feeling and expectation of the viewer dramatically. In the same way, the sound of a police siren off-screen signals the arrival of a police cruiser. When

- **Coverage:** filming multiple angles of the same scene
- **Two shot:** a shot that depicts two objects balanced on either side of the frame
- **Score:** instrumental music that is composed for a film
- **Soundtrack:** prerecorded songs that help enhance the overall film
- **Diegetic sound:** any sound that has a source within the world of the film; sound the characters on screen can hear
- **Nondiegetic sound:** sound, such as music or voice-over narration, that does not have a source in the story world
- **Omniscient narrator:** the disembodied voice that gives us information but doesn't belong to any of the characters in the film

the audience is presented with the cruiser itself, expectations have been satisfied. However, if the siren sound is followed by a shot of a hound dog, there will undoubtedly be questions.

Another powerful function of film sound is how it can give new meaning to silence and how silence gives new meaning to sound. Let us use the following example: In Francis Ford Coppola's (1979) *Apocalypse Now*, there is a scene in which Chef and Willard are off the boat and exploring the jungle, looking for mangoes. We are presented not only with a very quiet passage (no gun fire), but also with slow camera movement intended to add to the suspense. This silence forces us to anticipate that something will happen. So we concentrate on the screen, waiting. And bam! A tiger, roaring loudly, pops out of the jungle, almost from nowhere. In this instance, the silence sets up the suspense successfully.

When filming important scenes, like conversations, it is important to get **coverage**—multiple angles of the same scene. It is equally important for students to know that simple manipulation of sound is common, in fact necessary, in filmmaking. So, when directors shoot a conversation, they film it first in its entirety in a **two-shot**, medium close-up of the two characters. This is the audio that can be used for the entire scene no matter what shot they cut to by overlaying and synching it up to all of the other shots. Figure 7.1 shows an example of dialogue overlap. Obviously, it is crucial that the actors deliver the same lines in the same way with the same inflection and emphasis in every take, so it is important that they rehearse, rehearse, and rehearse!

The music for a film can be broken down into two categories: the score and the soundtrack. The **score** is typically instrumental music that is composed for a film. It adds emotion, cues characters and events, and tells the audience how to feel. The **soundtrack** is, typically, made up of prerecorded songs that help enhance the overall film. There are exceptions, of course. Some scores are arranged from pre-existing material just as some soundtracks are recorded specifically for a film. Table 7.1 lists some famous composers and the films they're known for.

One of the more important elements of film sound that students must understand is how sound works within a space. Because all sound comes from a source, we can point to the sound's exact origin to help us better understand the events in the film. Events that take place in the story world are considered **diegetic**. So, diegetic sound is sound that has a source in the story world, meaning the actors on screen can hear it. There is also **nondiegetic sound**, which is sound that comes from a source outside the story world; the characters onscreen cannot hear it. Music that's added to enhance the film's action and an **omniscient narrator**—the disembodied voice that gives us information but doesn't belong to any of the characters in the film—

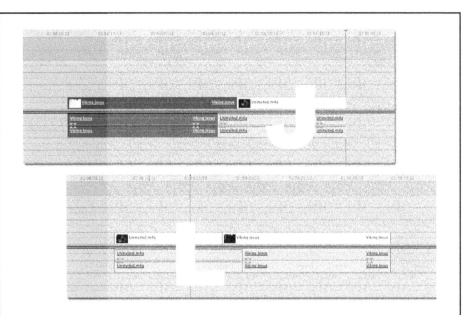

When filmmakers edit conversations in shot or reverse shot, they use a **dialogue overlap** to smooth down the visual change of shot. In a dialogue overlap, the filmmaker continues a line of dialogue across a cut. Editors use two different types of overlaps, J-cuts and L-cuts. J-cuts start the sound from the next shot while the first shot is still on screen. L-cuts maintain the sound from the first shot through the edit and over the beginning of the second shot.

FIGURE 7.1. DIALOGUE OVERLAP.

are the two most common uses of nondiegetic sound. The simplest way to understand this is to pick any sound and then ask, "Can any single character onscreen hear that sound?" If the answer is "yes," then the sound must be part of the **diegesis**, or a diegetic sound. If the answer is "no," the sound is considered nondiegetic.

As stated throughout this discourse on sound, off-screen sound can be an effective tool in a young filmmaker's bag of tricks. Because sound is so powerful, it can trigger an audience to believe something exists that truly doesn't. Let us revisit the idea of the police siren. If a director cues a sound of the siren from off-screen and flashes some red and blue lights on a character, the audience will assume that there is a policeman there and that the character is in big trouble. A police officer is never cast, a police cruiser is never used, and no money is spent on anything other than two flashing lights. By adding the sound of the siren in postproduction, it legitimizes the scene, making it much more realistic.

KEY TERM
- **Diegesis:** the world of the film's story; everything the characters onscreen can see and hear is part of the diegesis

TABLE 7.1
FAMOUS COMPOSERS

Composer	Films
Bernard Herrmann	*Psycho, Citizen Kane, Taxi Driver*
John Williams	*Star Wars, Jaws, Jurassic Park*
Ennio Morricone	*The Good, The Bad, and The Ugly; Once Upon a Time in the West*
Danny Elfman	*Pee-Wee's Big Adventure, Batman, The Nightmare Before Christmas*
Walter Murch	*The Conversation, Apocalypse Now, Cold Mountain*
Hans Zimmer	*Gladiator, The Dark Knight, Inception*
Jerry Goldsmith	*Alien, Star Trek, Chinatown*
James Horner	*Titanic, Avatar, Apollo 13*
Howard Shore	*Lord of the Rings, The Silence of the Lambs, The Hobbit*
Henry Mancini	*Touch of Evil, The Glenn Miller Story, The Pink Panther*
John Barry	*James Bond films, Born Free, Midnight Cowboy*
Michael Giacchino	*The Incredibles, Ratatouille, Up*
Elmer Bernstein	*The Magnificent Seven, The Blues Brothers, To Kill a Mockingbird*

Note: There are a few mistakes beginner filmmakers make with sound; the following anecdote comes from coauthor Uriah Donnelly:

My first year teaching high school filmmaking, I was speaking with a student who had helped someone shoot a film the previous year. She told me that while they were trying to record a scene where the main character gets an important phone call they couldn't get the phone to ring at the right time. They would call the phone from a cell phone, but the timing was never right. It never occurred to any of the cast and crew to just pretend the phone rang and add the sound effects later.

Similarly, I had another student shoot a pivotal dialogue scene in a car. Part of the scene incorporated music playing from the car stereo. Instead of recording the scene without the music, the student put the volume on low while they filmed their lines. The result: the audience couldn't make out large portions of the dialogue because of the white noise muddling their lines.

The study guide below is designed for a screening of Francis Ford Coppola's (1974) *The Conversation*. Some other suggested screenings that can be used as a similar exercise include:

- Beginner: *Wall-E* (Morris & Stanton, 2008)

- Intermediate: *Jurassic Park* (Kennedy, Molen, & Spielberg, 1993)

- Advanced: *Upstream Color* (Gooden, LeClair, Douglass, & Carruth, 2013); *Apocalypse Now** (Coppola, 1979)

STUDY GUIDE
LISTENING TO THE CONVERSATION

1. There are three classifications of sound in cinema: speech, music, and noise. What are some examples of each from *The Conversation* (Coppola, 1974)? Are there any instances when these categories mix? If so, to what effect?

2. When thinking about sound's spatial dimension in cinema, we must ask if it is part of the fictional world that is created by the film. Sound that the characters onscreen can hear is referred to as *diegetic*. So, nondiegetic sound refers to the sound that doesn't exist in that space; the characters on screen cannot hear it. What are some examples of nondiegetic sound? How does *The Conversation* use both auditory devices? How is it effective?

3. Sound is often used to convey feelings of horror, chaos, distress, etc. How does this film use sound to evoke emotion?

4. In cinema, fidelity refers to the extent to which the sound is faithful to the source as we conceive it. If we hear a train whistle, we expect to see a train onscreen. Does *The Conversation* stay faithful to this expectation? How?

A CLOSING EXERCISE

If your A/V equipment allows for it, this exercise can be quite helpful in articulating to students the power of music in film. Start by accessing the opening sequence of *The Shining* (Kubrick, 1980) or some other film with an ambiguous enough opening. Select three different songs to play on another device. Screen the clip with the volume muted and repeat it each time while selecting a random song from the three. After all have been used, watch the original version with the volume up. In order to stimulate discussion, a good question to ask after each viewing is, "What genre of movie is this?" You will be surprised at the variety of answers given. Therein lies the point. The music dictated the understanding.

Following the exercise, it is important to stress to students that when they work with adding music to their own films, they must be careful in their song selection. Ideally, creating new music or utilizing music that their peers have composed is the best option. The temptation to plop any old song into their films can get tricky. An audience always listens to the lyrics and will try to make connections between what they see and hear.

THE DOCUMENTARY

We have introduced you to many genres in the previous chapters, but there is one that has been purposefully left out until now. The reason is that the type of filmmaking known as the **documentary** requires a different perspective on the craft. Rather than offering a fictional story for the audience to enjoy, a documentary film is one that is characterized as nonfiction and seeks to "document" a facet of life, either to teach or record a historical person or person(s), place(s), or event(s).

Documentary films often provide opinions or messages intended for the audience. The directors and writers of a documentary film take great care in utilizing primary sources, such as photographs, historical and contemporary film footage, interviews, and documents. The documentary form has its roots in early newsreels and newscasts of the 1920s, and even now, modern news programs follow a similar format. Not too long after, the emergence of propaganda films (films that are meant to persuade a large audience), started to be produced. Leni Riefenstahl's 1935 *Triumph of the Will*, which recounted the 1934 Nazi Party Congress is one of our personal favorites for its nature and style of filmmaking. Similarly in the U.S., the Why We Fight series was commissioned by the United States government to help keep up morale for the American soldiers.

In recent times, documentaries have become more popular and accessible. *March of the Penguins* (Darondeau, Lioud, Priou, Jacquet, 2005) and *An Inconvenient Truth* (Bender, Burns, David, & Guggenheim, 2006) have set the stage for many other films in this genre. *The Civil War* (Burns, 1990), *Baseball* (Novick & Burns, 1994), and *The National Parks: America's Best Idea* (Duncan & Burns, 2009), all directed by Ken Burns, are excellent films to show clips from. They define the modern documentary.

TYPES OF DOCUMENTARIES

There are many ways to separate the types of documentary filmmaking, but for our purposes we can categorize them into three different types. Poetic documentaries integrate images and music in an experimental and lyrical way, blending and overlapping images intended for the complete enjoyment of the viewer. Expository documentaries seek to offer an objective look at an event or events in history and are often narrated. Observational documentaries offer a blend of the poetic and expository approaches. By utilizing unscripted footage of real-life events, the directors can often infuse commentary and narration, or may even reenact events.

SOME STYLES IN A DOCUMENTARY

In order to break down the elements of a documentary, it is important to look at two different aspects, the visual and the audio. Film footage may be images of individuals being interviewed, live footage that captures real life or reenacted scenes, or filler material such as a sunset, beach, or forest scene. The audience may also be shown charts or graphs. There is usually the appearance of text, either in the form of words introducing a scene, phrases, quotes, or subtitles. In some cases, animation is utilized.

The audio track of a documentary can contain narration, either on- or off-screen, sounds from the real world (e.g., cars, crowds, conversations), or music used to enhance the emotional quality of the footage. As with a traditional film, selections may be prerecorded music or scored. Sound effects are also quite common, and silence is often used.

Editing and transitions also play a large part in the structure of a documentary. Focusing on parts of still images, wiping from scene to scene, and the use of cuts and visual effects are used just as in traditional filmmaking and are used with intention. There are many venues available for access to documentaries. The streaming outlets of Netflix, Amazon, Apple TV, and Hulu provide a documentary on just about every topic, and many will appeal to your students. There are two benefits to this. The first is that it provides a cross-curricular connection to any of the disciplines in your school (e.g., math, science, history, language arts, technology, etc.). The second is that many of the state and national academic and creative contests (e.g., History Day, Destination Imagination) offer a documentary as a product choice. Let us look at the following series of activities intended to instruct students through the process of creating a historical documentary. The study guide below is designed for a screening of Errol Morris's (1988) *The Thin Blue Line*. This documentary provides a great example of a form in which information unfolds over time, and by the end hooks the entire audience. Other suggested screenings include:

- *March of the Penguins* (Darondeau, Lioud, Priou, & Jacquet, 2005)
- *Spellbound* (Welch & Blitz, 2002)
- *Supersize Me* (Spurlock, 2004)

STUDY GUIDE
THE THIN BLUE LINE

1. This documentary argues that a man, Randall Adams, was wrongfully convicted of murder in Dallas County, Texas. In your opinion, where do filmmaker Errol Morris's sympathies lie? What specific scenes would you point to in defending your answer?

2. How would you describe the documentary techniques Morris uses to make his case? Is this what you expected to see in a documentary? Why or why not?

3. A blue line or stripe is a symbol used by law enforcement to commemorate fallen officers. Why did Errol Morris choose "*The Thin Blue Line*" as the title of his film? Also, during the opening credits of the film, the title appears and the word blue turns to red. What may be the significance of this?

DOCUMENTARY PROJECT

The following project, Utilizing Primary Sources to Create a Documentary, can be adapted for any major event or situation that your geographic area has had to or is currently dealing with. In completing the work for the project, students will learn to recognize the difference between a primary and secondary source, conduct further research using primary source information, engage in discussions relating to the effects of a major event or situation, conduct oral history interviews, and possibly present the finished product to an audience. The various aspects of the project requires the following materials and activities:

- field trips to various locations in and around the local geographic area,
- one or two video cameras/tripod,
- a computer with editing program,
- a still camera, and
- a digital scanner.

The project begins with an introduction to the differences between primary and secondary sources. Students will be given a variety of materials they must sort through, identifying which would be characterized as primary and which would be secondary. Once this is complete, the students should possess a strong understanding of the differences. Students may already know the difference between the two.

With most or all of the students having grown up in or around your particular area, it is assumed that many of them will have a working knowledge of a particular event or situation of current or historical significance (e.g, a natural disaster, political event, or major news story). Even more important is that many students will have older relatives who were alive during a particular historical event and can remember with great detail or have materials that were kept as keepsakes.

Students are then instructed to brainstorm a list of primary sources that may be available to them in order to develop a complete understanding of the events that took place, apart from the usual books and special newspaper editions. The list might contain the following:

- newspaper interviews from the days following the event,
- obituaries from the same time,
- news radio recordings and possible television reports,
- personal diaries and letters written by relatives,
- insurance claims of the time,
- facts and figures relating to the event,
- photographs,
- recorded oral histories of living relatives, or
- locations in the area to visit, with possible memorials and plaques.

Once the students have compiled a list, it is then time to think about where they might go to find these resources. The list below provides some instruction on what should occur and what the students need to be aware of:

- a trip to a city or neighborhood public library in order to access public records, microfilm, microfiche, photo archives, and newspaper archives;
- a trip to a city or neighborhood historical society to explore the archives;
- a walking trip around a city or neighborhood in order to see actual locations that were the scene of the event or events;
- online searches for information;
- recorded or filmed interviews with a family member; or
- a visit by an invited speaker.

After this series of information-gathering activities, the students will then generate lists of good questions to ask the people who agree to be interviewed. The entire class can then settle on a bank of questions to be used in the process. These will relate to the overall interest that the students have about the event and what they wish to know. The goal is that by this time, the students will have developed a sense of autonomy, acting on their own with little instruction. It is their work, their project, their commitment.

When all the discussions have taken place regarding what they want to know, students are to develop a plan for the documentary. This includes the selection of various jobs required for the project. If you are working with a large class, you may wish to have two to three teams of students working with the same class materials. This way, they will produce two to three different compositions of the same event. If the population of students that you are working with is small, then each can take on one of the following roles:

- narration writer,
- narration reader for voice-over work,
- video camera people to film the interviews,
- interviewers,
- video editors,
- photo experts and photo scanners, and
- a director.

Once jobs have been assigned based on interest, the students can begin work on the production. They meet as a group to discuss what they need to accomplish. Handouts 8.1 and 8.2 are provided to help your students plan out the documentary. The Narrative Template (Handout 8.1) seeks to have students describe their project, propose or list any budget items, determine a project schedule, and list who is responsible for what task. Also included are potential audiences. The Documentary Shooting Script Template (Handout 8.2) will be used for mapping out shots and still images, along with potential voice-over narrative. It would be beneficial to have a whole-class meeting for the first and last 5 minutes of class in order to get a sense of where each group starts and finishes. Filming of interviews can be conducted either during school time or at a time agreed upon by all.

After all the pieces are acquired and completed, the director, along with the video editors, set to work on the actual documentary. They utilize each part worked on, scan photos and documents, create titles and acquire music, record voice-overs, import interviews, create credits that reference all primary sources, and edit the entire film together. The final work should be between 20–30 minutes in length.

While the directors and editors are busy, the other students could work in the area of public relations, creating flyers, posters, and planning when the viewing will take place. The final product could be screened in the classroom and posted online for further dissemination, premiered in the evening as part of a school event, or even entered into a student contest. The list that follows includes some great resources for conducting historical research and creating documentaries that you may wish to utilize:

- *Looking for Data in All the Right Places* by Alane J. Starko and Gina D. Schack (1992)
- *Research Comes Alive!* by and Gina D. Schack (1998)
- *Creating History Documentaries* by Deborah Escobar (2001)
- *The Oral History Manual* by Barbara W. Sommer and Mary Kay Quinlan (2009)

HANDOUT 8.1

NARRATIVE TEMPLATE

Project Description

```
[empty box]
```

Budget

```
[empty box]
```

Project Schedule

```
[empty box]
```

Collaboration

```
[empty box]
```

Population to Benefit (Potential Audiences)

```
[empty box]
```

Name: _____ Date: _____

DOCUMENTARY SHOOTING
SCRIPT TEMPLATE

Director: _____

Film: _____

Timecode	Video	Audio

CHAPTER 9

THE FINAL PROJECT

With the previous chapters in the rearview for you and your students, the possibility exists for the planning, producing, and screening of an original work by the class. Throughout this text we have tried to supply you with the instruction needed to offer your students the tools needed to successfully complete a longer film project. Depending on your educational environment (e.g., one-day workshop, week-long camp, quarter, semester, yearlong enrichment, or before- or afterschool activity), the introduction of the chapters in this text and the creation of a final project can be done in a few ways. If your program is a full-year course, you could begin by introducing the steps of this project throughout the presentation of the chapters.

The topic, subject, style, genre, and length of the films created during this time are up to you, and as stated before, are dependent on the time you have to work with your students. In addition to the direct instruction found in this text, these assignments provide a more specific and in-depth look at the pre- and postproduction process. They can be tweaked, edited, or even eliminated as part of your own individual process.

Let us look at the following initial project as an example, which you could easily use at the starting-off point for having students experience the process of filmmaking for themselves. Its inception was at the Beacon Charter High School for the Arts in Woonsocket,

RI, where students were instructed to make a 10-minute autobiographical film in whatever genre they wished. Some students made documentaries, others made biopics, and some made experimental films or fictional narratives that touched on subjects important to their lives. Although there are many restrictions embedded in the directions, there should never be a limit on creativity.

Each of the exercises below can be used for a variety of formats and project types. They cover each and every aspect of filmmaking covered in the text and illustrate the steps one would have to go through when working on a professional project.

EXERCISE 1: THE INITIAL THOUGHTS

Students are instructed to write down ideas for their films. If your class size is large, you may want to have them each submit an idea and then vote on them in class. You may also want to wait for the voting until after the second or third exercises so that all students can receive the training offered in them first. Students should also be encouraged to come up with as many ideas as they can. To get the ideas flowing, posing questions like "What kind of film do I want to make? and "What do I want to 'tell' people?" will help.

You could also have your students imagine that an audience member is entering the theater to see their film. What is the first image they see? What do they hear? What feelings/emotions are immediate to the audience?

EXERCISE 2: THE LOGLINE

Once an idea is decided upon, have the students sum up their story in 25 words or less. This is the creation of a logline. The logline should not include detail like a character's name; instead it should read like a summary that captures the concept and feeling of your film. For example:

> After a twister transports a lonely Kansas farm girl to a magical land, she sets out on a dangerous journey to find a wizard with the power to send her home. (*The Wizard of Oz*; LeRoy & Fleming, 1939)

> After learning his father was murdered, a brooding prince struggles with whether or not to kill the culprit, his uncle—the new king. (*Hamlet*; Olivier, 1948)

Questions to consider include:

- 🎬 Who is the main character and what does he/she want?
- 🎬 Who or what is standing in the way of the main character?
- 🎬 What makes this story unique?

EXERCISE 3: THREE SENTENCES

At this point, you may want to have the students submit or share their loglines with the class. A few of them could be selected through voting and these will be used for the subsequent exercises, which will require group work and dynamics. Whether individually or as a group, students are directed to turn their logline into three sentences. This can be completed in a couple of ways. All are very good methods, and if time permits, you could offer all three as separate exercises. Below are some tips:

- 🎬 Have students come up with a beginning, middle, and end for their story. What's the first major event? The second? What's the final event?
- 🎬 Have the students break their narrative down into three parts: introduction, major conflict, resolution.
- 🎬 Students could develop bookends for their story. In this way, the first and third parts frame the second part in the form of flashback or some other storytelling device.

EXERCISE 4: THREE
PARAGRAPHS/SCENE LIST

Once the students have their three sentences, they will need to expand these into three paragraphs, where detail, including character names and setting, are developed and included. Students are asked to begin thinking visually! Some of your students will have this done quickly while others may take their time and flesh out a wealth of detail.

When the three paragraphs are complete, students can then begin to create a scene list, always keeping the major events of the narrative in mind. If time permits or their enthusiasm is too great, they may even begin to write out important chunks of dialogue. Remember, though, that the main goal here is for the story to have a distinct beginning, middle, and end.

EXERCISE 5: THE SCRIPT

Once the individual student or groups of students have developed their idea into three paragraphs, it is time for them to begin writing the first draft of the script. The process of screenwriting, as detailed in Chapter 4, can be a lengthy process, for scripts often go through multiple drafts.

Given your situation in the classroom, work through three drafts of your students' scripts: first draft, second draft, and final draft or shooting script. These may be completed on a word processing program, through a script program, or online in a Google Docs environment. Regardless, as the educator it will be up to you to read and comment on each one, providing ideas, suggestions, and corrections.

Students can sometimes become very frustrated when they get their scripts returned. Usually, the first draft will be marked up considerably and this can often lead to feelings of low self-efficacy (e.g., dejection and rejection). At this time, it is good to remind students that ALL scripts go through multiple drafts and even the most seasoned writer needs an editor. Obviously, each draft should be more refined than the last, with the final draft being as error free as possible. When the final drafts have been handed in, let the students know that they are not done, for the preparation has only just begun.

EXERCISE 6: STORYBOARDING

Storyboards are important tools for those wishing to visually relay an idea to the entire cast and crew. Having students create storyboards to draw out major portions of their film allows them to visualize their shots before filming. By drawing out actions, angles, shot distances, and more, they are, in a sense, "shooting the film" before actually shooting the film. Think of the storyboard as a visual script. Obviously, not every student comes in with the same level of artistic skill. Storyboarding takes a great deal of time and patience, so if you or your students do not have one or both of these, storyboarding could be skipped.

However, it is incredibly important for students to start thinking visually, and storyboarding is great way to accomplish that. Instead of having the students storyboard the entire script, they could pick out two or three important scenes and do their best to capture, in the storyboard sheets provided, what their film will look like. Samples of storyboard sheets can be found in Appendix C.

EXERCISE 7: PRODUCTION BREAKDOWN REPORTS

Production breakdown reports (PBRs), or production call sheets, are essential as students prepare to go on location to shoot. Have them think of them as checklists, ensuring that they have everything needed to be successful during filming. Included in the PBRs are lists for cast, props, costumes, equipment, and any other important items needed during filming.

Because filmmakers shoot multiple scenes in one day, regardless of where the scenes take place in the narrative, production breakdown reports help organize everything you need for each location. See the PBR template in the appendix.

ADDITIONAL EXERCISES: THE ANIMATIC, OVERHEAD DIAGRAMS, AND THE SHOT LIST

THE ANIMATIC

An animatic is a fun way for students to see their script come to life before actually picking up a camera. This project involves taking the storyboards created in the last assignment and scanning them into a computer, cropping each frame into a singular image, and then placing the images into the timeline of an editing program. Students can also add sound and dialogue or may use a paint program to colorize their stills. The animatic is a great way for students to see their films play out narratively. The following YouTube videos provide excellent examples of animatics:

- 🎬 http://www.youtube.com/watch?v=-2JcnCpXexM
- 🎬 http://www.youtube.com/watch?v=AEjzvMx0R_0

OVERHEAD DIAGRAMS

Overhead diagrams make use of major scenes. In thinking of everything involved—characters, props, and cameras—the students proceed to create a "map" with an overhead viewpoint. This not only helps all involved to understand how the scene is blocked, but more importantly, is used to understand where the cameras need to be placed in order to capture the shots your students have imagined. The website for the film *The Honeysting* (Miller, Emiliani, & Lewin, 2009; http://thehoneysting.com) has a few great examples of both storyboards and overhead diagrams.

THE SHOT LIST

The shot list presents each shot that will appear in the finished film. Much like the production breakdown report, the shot list involves the listing of each major scene and then groups together the shots that will need to be captured on the same day and/or in the same location regardless of when the event being filmed takes place in your narrative. For example, if the beginning scene of the film takes place at a bus stop and the ending scene does, too, both should be shot at the same time. One location, two scenes.

The shot list, and the understanding that scenes of a film do not have to be shot in the order they are written, is, at times, a hard concept for the students to grasp. This is especially true for the actors. Students should include the following items in their shot list:

- scene shot number,
- camera set-up (i.e., shot distance and angle),
- camera movement,
- character blocking (e.g., where are the characters in the frame, whether is there movement), and
- dialogue or major action.

See the example in Table 9.1. It is important to note that you could include multiple lines of dialogue for the same shot.

A great exercise for the students to complete at this time is the backward shot list. This involves students working in groups, who choose a scene from a movie they already know and work to break down each shot in order. The direction is simple; every time there's a cut, a new line is created. The scene, shot, blocking, and dialogue entries will be the easiest to enter, but students will also have to identify camera distance (i.e., scale), angle, and movement. This could be done as a class exercise with one screened scene, as groups of students with devices to watch downloaded or streamed films, or as an individual assignment for homework. Simply use the table format in Microsoft Word or comparable spreadsheet program and create a table or chart. You could even create a template like the one in Table 9.2 that can be shared.

FILMING

At this point, the students can begin to prepare for the filming of scenes. They have now acquired all of the tools needed for preproduction. When each of the exercises are complete and materials gathered, you and your students can venture out to the locations for filming.

Living in the digital age of film has its benefits. Instead of using film that needs to be developed and edited by manual splicing, capturing footage now doesn't cost more than the most expensive Secure Digital (SD) card. We do not have to be concerned with unintentionally wasting money by overshooting. Very rarely is the first "take" or filming of a shot perfect. Have the students repeat the filming at least three times. This will ensure a good "take," or at least will provide the students with plenty of options.

Completing filming as independent projects or as afterschool activities will allow you and your students to enjoy an open time to film, and in many cases students or groups of students will film in the evening or on weekends. If you have chosen this curriculum as an in-school enrichment exercise, then most likely you will be forced to work inside of a specific schedule and will need to schedule ahead for time to allow for filming. It is easier to work with multiple groups during this time, as many of them may share similar locations, and may even utilize the same large and small props. Scheduling may also be dependent on what equipment is available. Again, students may be using their own cameras or devices or may bring them in to school for use, but you will need to at least have the following on hand:

- a digital recording camera or device,
- a tripod, and
- a memory card for the camera (at least 8 GB). *Hint:* Setting the camera to record to the memory card ensures that the footage can be uploaded to any computer.

Before your students head out, either on their own or during school, groups should be told that they need to be responsible, respectful, and ready to work. Stress that they must remain aware of their surroundings at all times. This includes preexisting light sources and natural sounds. For example, the film *Caddyshack* (Kenney & Ramis, 1980) had quite a bit of dif-

TABLE 9.1
SHOT LIST

Scene Number/ Shot Number	Scale (Shot)	Angle	Camera Move	Character Blocking	Dialogue or Action
1/1	MCU	Low angle	Camera pans left	Frankie leans against the jukebox	Frankie: "I love this tune, man!"

TABLE 9.2
BACKWARD SHOT LIST

Scene Number/ Shot Number	Time Code [MM:SS]	Scale (Shot)	Angle	Camera Move	Character Blocking	Dialogue or Action
1/1	00:00	LS, CU	H/L	Dolly, pan	CHAR moves l/r	"I fell!"
1/2						
1/3						
1/4						
1/5						
1/6						
1/7						
1/8						

ficulty in production because the golf course where they shot was next to an airport. Multiple times, takes were ruined by the sound of planes overhead.

Other exterior shooting concerns that students are challenged with include the wind and the sun. What may seem like a light breeze to them will actually translate as a hurricane whipping through the microphone. The use of a boom microphone with a wind guard could help, as will well-hidden lapel microphones, but these might not be an option. Although the sun provides great natural light to exterior shots, it can be difficult to avoid and manipulate the shadows it casts. Backlighting can present another issue when shooting on a day when the sun is high and hot. A character standing with the sun behind him or her will appear completely blacked out onscreen. Tell the students to always shoot with the sun at their back, if possible. The best time to shoot outside is when the sky is a bit overcast and the sun is hidden behind the clouds. Some other tips that may seem obvious but should be mentioned include:

- Borrowed equipment: If equipment is borrowed, make sure to keep a sign-out sheet and if your students are taking equipment home, have them return it the next day, even if they need it the next night.

- If you are working directly with your students, try to stay out of the process as much as possible, offering advice only when asked. Students seem to ask fewer questions when they are allowed to figure something out for themselves.

DEADLINES

If footage is not shot during school hours, then there must be some deadlines to adhere to. If time permits, students could screen their "raw" footage to the class or assigned groups. This will essentially be the first **crit** (short for critique), where students show their work to their peers and get feedback. Criticism, when spoken in positive and productive ways, can be a very valuable resource for filmmakers. Instruct students to be critical in their responses by careful and exact consideration of the work at hand. That means they need to look at all components of their film: aesthetics, technique, and content. Emphasize that the critique process is never one of a personal nature. It is practiced to make your work stronger, more creative, and better crafted. Some students, after viewing their footage, may want to go back out and reshoot some scenes, but if time is through for filming, it can be considered more or less in the can at this point.

THE ROUGH CUT

If students are working at home, plan on a due date and leave them to their experiences. If you are working in school, the following is a suggestion of how to manage multiple projects at one time.

Once all of the footage is shot, the students should upload the footage into an editing program. It is important that students continue to be organized in this process. Footage should be named and kept in folders, either by scene, shot type, date, or some other organizing factor. The more organized the footage is, the easier it will be to find once the editing begins. Depending on the technology used, the time it takes to edit will vary.

Try to remove yourself as much as possible from the editing process. Directions from you should involve a few creative reminders and suggestions to students for how to pace their work time. Many of the programs have great "help" features that can guide the students, or you can provide instruction through tutorials. The beauty of working with digital footage is that the original material will not be compromised, and so mistakes—and there will be some—are fine to make. Many programs also have an autosave feature that saves the day if the computer freezes.

If time permits, another crit could follow at this time, before the fine-tuning. The feedback on students' progress by you and their peers might persuade them to change a scene or move something around.

THE FINAL CUT

After the first round of editing, it is a good idea to remind the students to go back through and clean up all of the shots. This requires cutting specific footage by a fraction of a second to ensure that the edits are crisp. Students may also need to utilize certain effects and transitions. These are readily available on all programs. Titles and credits may also need to be added at the beginning and end. Students can begin to insert sound effects, record voice-overs, and curate soundtrack elements.

Remind them to ask questions when needed, and let them know you can assist them if possible. The use of earphones during the editing process is highly recommend. Multiple computers with random sounds can be disruptive.

SCREENING

The big payoff. Once the dust has settled, and everyone can relax, it is time to screen the work that your students have labored hard on for so long. Students will revel in the feeling of seeing their work up on the big screen, and this big screen could be a TV or smartboard in the classroom, an auditorium or school theater, or even a local theater or hall. Invite parents, relatives, and friends. Have them share in the excitement. Make it an event.

Students could also choose to enter an original screenplay or film/video into a contest or film festival. Many independent filmmakers find funding from friends and family. Nowadays with online community outreach like Kickstarter and Indiegogo, aspiring filmmakers can solicit financial help from people all over the world. There are also federal and state grant opportunities in certain states that can be tapped as a resource to help fund various projects.

CHAPTER 10

THAT'S A WRAP

Well, as they say in the film industry, "That's a wrap." In truth, it is only the beginning for you and your students. We estimate that there are over ten thousand books on the study of filmmaking, film production, screenwriting, and associated subjects. Each author has his or her point of view, words of advice and wisdom, and a specific audience with whom to speak. After all, the filmmaking medium is more than 100 years old. One text alone cannot begin to cover all that is known about the art, or begin to train students in all of the skills needed.

Think of this text as an introduction to the world of filmmaking from a student's perspective. Through each and every chapter, you have guided them through the main facets of the discipline, introduced some classic directors and films, and offered the opportunity for them to create their own work. Nothing could be better than that.

There are many texts and programs to choose from when searching for a guide for you and your students into the world of film and filmmaking. There are two web-based curricula that we would like to share with you. They are quite extensive and bulky (something we have tried to avoid); however, they are comprehensive and there are many mini-exercises, lessons, and suggestions for films to explore.

- The Film Foundation: http://www.storyofmovies.org/common/110 41/curriculum.cfm?clientID=11041&QID=6661

- Moviestorm: https://www.moviestorm.co.uk/hub/teaching/ education_lesson_plans

We wish you the best as you continue to explore the world of cinema! Have fun.

REFERENCES

Arndt, S. (Producer), & Tykwer, T. (Director). (1998). *Run Lola run* [Motion picture]. Germany: Sony Pictures Classics.

Baron, F. Brown, M. (Producers), & Luhrmann, B. (Producer and Director). (2001). *Moulin Rouge!* [Motion picture]. United Kingdom/Australia/United States: 20th Century Fox.

Bender, L., Burns, S., David, L. (Producers), & Guggenheim, D. (Director). (2006). *An inconvenient truth* [Motion picture]. United States: Paramount Classics.

Berbert, M. (Producer), & Truffaut, F. (Director). (1973). *Day for night* [Motion picture]. France: Columbia Pictures/Warner Brothers.

Bernstein, S. (Producer), & Hitchcock, A. (Director). (1948). *Rope* [Motion picture]. United States: Warner Brothers/Universal Pictures.

Brown, D., Tolkin, M., Wechsler, N. (Producers), & Altman, R. (Director). (1992). *The player* [Motion picture]. United States: Fine Line Features/Pathé.

Burk, B., & Spielberg, S. (Producers), & Abrams, J. J. (Producer and Director). (2011). *Super 8* [Motion picture]. United States. Paramount Pictures.

Burns, K. (Producer and Director). (1990). *The Civil War* [Documentary series]. United States: Public Broadcasting System.

Cage, N., Levine, J., (Producers), & Merhige, E. E. (Director). (2000). *Shadow of the vampire* [Motion picture]. United States: Lions Gate Films.

Canton, N., Gale, B. (Producers), & Zemeckis, R. (Director). (1985). *Back to the future* [Motion picture]. United States: Universal Pictures.

Charlot, G. (Producer), & Truffaut, F. (Producer and Director). (1959). *The 400 blows* [Motion picture]. France: Cocinor.

Coen, E. (Producer), & Coen, J. (Director). (2000). *O brother, where art thou?* [Motion picture]. United States: Touchstone Pictures.

Coppola, F. F. (Producer and Director). (1974). *The conversation* [Motion picture]. United States: Paramount Pictures.

Coppola, F. F. (Producer and Director). (1979). *Apocalypse now* [Motion picture]. United States: United Artists.

Darondeau, Y., Lioud, C., Priou, E. (Producers), & Jacquet, L. (Director). (2005). *March of the penguins* [Motion picture]. France: Buena Vista International/Warner Independent Pictures.

Dashiell, C. (2000). The oldest movies. Retrieved from http://www.cinescene.com/dash/lumiere.html

Deeley, M. (Producer), & Scott, R. (Director). (1982). *Blade runner* [Motion picture]. United States: Warner Bros.

DeSylva, B., Sistrom, J. (Producers), & Wilder, B. (Director). (1944). *Double indemnity* [Motion picture]. United States: Paramount Pictures/Universal Studios.

Di Novi, D., (Producer), & Burton, T. (Producer and Director). (1990). *Edward Scissorhands* [Motion picture]. United States: 20th Century Fox.

Disney, W. (Producer), & Stevenson, R. (Director). (1964). *Mary Poppins* [Motion Picture]. United States: Walt Disney Productions.

Duncan, D. (Producer), & Burns, K. (Producer and Director). (2009). *The national parks: America's best idea* [Documentary series]. United States: Public Broadcasting System.

Escobar, D. (2001). *Creating history documentaries*. Waco, TX: Prufrock Press.

Field, S. (2005). *Screenplay: The foundations of screenwriting*. New York, NY: Delta.

Flinn, D. M. (1999). *How not to write a screenplay: 101 common mistakes most screenwriters make*. New York, NY: Lone Eagle.

Freed, A. (Producer), & Kelly, G., & Donen, S. (Directors). (1952). *Singin' in the rain* [Motion picture]. United States: Metro-Goldwyn-Mayer.

Gooden, C., LeClair, B., Douglass, S. (Producers), & Carruth, S. (Producer and Director). (2013). *Upstream color* [Motion picture]. United States: ERBP

Heyman, D. (Producer), & Columbus, C. (Director). (2001). *Harry Potter and the sorcerer's stone* [Motion Picture]. United Kingdom/United States: Warner Brothers.

Hitchcock, A. (Producer and Director). (1946). *Notorious* [Motion picture]. United States: RKO Radio Pictures.

Hitchcock, A. (Producer and Director). (1951). *Strangers on a train* [Motion picture]. United States: Warner Brothers.

Hitchcock, A. (Producer and Director). (1960). *Psycho* [Motion picture]. United States: Paramount Pictures/Universal Pictures.

Hunter, L. (2004). *Lew Hunter's screenwriting 434: The industry's premier teacher reveals the secrets of the successful screenplay.* New York, NY: Perigree Trade.

Iglesias, K. (2011). *The 101 habits of highly successful screenwriters: Insider secrets from Hollywood's top writers.* Blue Ash, OH: Adams Media.

Kennedy, K., Molen, G. R. (Producers), & Spielberg, S. (Director). (1993). *Jurassic park* [Motion picture]. United States: Universal Pictures.

Kenney, D. (Producer), & Ramis, H. (Director). (1980). *Caddyshack* [Motion picture]. United States: Warner Brothers Pictures.

King, G., Headington, T., Depp, J. (Producers), & Scorsese, M. (Producer and Director). (2011). *Hugo* [Motion picture]. United States: Paramount Pictures.

Kubrick, S. (Producer and Director). (1980). *The shining* [Motion picture]. United States: Warner Bros.

Kurtz, G. (Producer), & Lucas, G. (Director). (1977). *Star wars episode IV: A new hope* [Motion picture]. United States: 20th Century Fox.

LeRoy, M. (Producer), & Fleming, V. (Director). (1939). *The wizard of Oz* [Motion picture]. United States: Metro-Goldwyn-Mayer.

Lipson, M. (Producer), & Morris, E. (Director). (1988). *The thin blue line* [Motion picture]. United States: Miramax Films/Umbrella Entertainment.

Méliès, G. (Producer and Director). (1902). *A trip to the moon* [Motion picture]. France: Star Film Company.

Miller, M., Emiliani, N. (Producers), & Lewin, A. S. (Director). (2009). *The honeysting* [Motion picture]. United States: Top Dog Films.

Morris, J. (Producer), & Stanton, A. (Director). (2008). *Wall-E* [Motion picture]. United States: Walt Disney Studios Motion Pictures.

Novick, L. (Producer), & Burns, K. (Producer and Director). (1994). *Baseball* [Documentary series]. United States: Public Broadcasting System.

Olivier, L. (Producer and Director). (1948). *Hamlet* [Motion picture]. United Kingdom: Rank Film Distributors/Universal Pictures.

Phillips, J., Phillips, M. (Producers), & Spielberg, S. (Director). (1977). *Close encounters of the third kind* [Motion picture]. United States: Columbia Pictures.

Renoir, C., Jay, J. (Producers), & Renoir, J. (Director). (1939). *The rules of the game* [Motion picture]. France: The Gaumont Film Company/Les Grands Films Classiques.

Riefenstahl, L. (Producer and Director). (1935). *Triumph of the will* [Motion Picture]. Germany: Universum Film AG.

Rivera, J. (Producer), & Docter, P. (Director). (2009). *Up* [Motion picture]. United States: Walt Disney Pictures.

Roven, C. (Producer), & Gilliam, T. (Director). (1995). *12 monkeys* [Motion picture]. United States: Universal Pictures.

Rudin, S., Rales, S., Dawson, J. (Producers), & Anderson, W. (Producer and Director). (2012). *Moonrise kingdom* [Motion picture]. United States: Focus Features.

Rudin, S., Stone, M. (Producers), & Parker, T. (Producer and Director). (2004). *Team America: World police* [Motion picture]. United States: Paramount Pictures.

Schack, G. D. (1998). *Research comes alive!* Waco, TX: Prufrock Press.

Sommer, B. W., & Quinlan, M. K. (2009). *The oral history manual.* Lanham, MD: AltaMira.

Sproxton, D. (Producer), Lord, Pl., & Park, N. (Producers and Directors). (2000). *Chicken run* [Motion picture]. United Kingdom/United States: Pathé/Dreamworks Pictures.

Spurlock, M. (Producer and Director). (2004). *Supersize me* [Motion picture]. United States: Samuel Goldwyn Films/Roadside Attractions

Starko, A. J., & Schack, G. D. (1992). *Looking for data in all the right places.* Waco, TX: Prufrock Press.

Thomas, E., Roven, C. (Producers), & Nolan, C. (Producer and Director). (2008). *The dark knight* [Motion picture]. United Kingdom/United States: Warner Bros.

Trottier, D. *The screenwriter's bible: A complete guide to writing, formatting, and selling your script* (6th ed.). Los Angeles, CA: Silman-James Press.

Welch, S. (Producer), & Blitz, J. (Producer and Director). (2002). *Spellbound* [Motion picture]. United States: ThinkFilm.

Welles, O. (Producer and Director). (1941). *Citizen Kane* [Motion picture]. United States: Mercury Productions.

Welles, O. (Producer and Director). (1958). *Touch of evil* [Motion picture]. United States: Universal Pictures.

Whitney, C. V. (Producer), & Ford, J. (Director). (1956). *The searchers* [Motion picture]. United States: Warner Brothers.

Zanuck, R. D., Brown, D. (Producers), & Spielberg, S. (Director). (1975). *Jaws* [Motion picture]. United States: Universal Pictures.

CROSS-CURRICULAR ACTIVITIES AND PROJECT IDEAS

Filmmaking involves a variety of disciplines, and as a result can lead to a host of discussions and activities related to many of the traditional school subject areas. What follows are short exercises intended to have the students see that no matter where their interest lies, there is something for them to contribute in the area of film production. They increase in depth and level of understanding and conclude with the suggestion of three larger independent projects.

SCIENCE

Obtain some old 16-mm or 35-mm film reels and film. Have the students observe the filmstrip itself; discuss that film is actually made of chemicals. Grab a book on film process and development from the local library and have the students find out how film is made, exposed, and developed.

Light and lenses play an important role in film and digital cameras. Check out a physics website or book and learn about light and lenses and see how they relate to film. If possible, gather some old broken camera parts or loose lenses. Have the students create a fact sheet that shows the principles of light and lenses. Put in a call to the local photo-developing store (if there are any left) or nearby college (most still have darkrooms) and ask if you take some students in to view the process of developing.

MATH

There is a difference between 8-mm, 16-mm, and 35-mm film cameras and film. Have the students explore the film itself and they will see the difference in sizes. Check out some books and access websites to share the mathematical differences between them. What does the size mean? Have the students write down five word problems relating to the different kinds of film speeds, and pick some peers to take the test.

Math is also used in calculating distances when filming in order to get the best shot. This is called focal distance and a director of photography needs to know lots of equations. Access some resources and try to find out what these equations are and what they tell you. Afterward, prepare a chart based on focal lengths and distances. You might want to obtain some light meters and tape measures.

Students could also conduct a survey about which kind of movies their friends and family prefer. They could then calculate the mean, average, and standard deviation and present this information in chart form.

HISTORY/BUSINESS

Throughout history, many things about film have changed. Styles of cameras, genres of filmmaking, impact on society, cost of moviemaking, and types of film have all evolved. Present a list of topics and have the students pick one and research it.

Professional film productions cost a lot of money. Have the students find budget breakdown data of a blockbuster film or an independent/student film. What, on average, is most of the money spent on in creating a film from start to finish? Have the students try to find out what it would cost to make a small-budget film during the summer.

Call your local or state film commission and ask for an interview or possible Skype or in-class visit with the director or see if he or she can provide you with a list of local filmmakers, many of whom would be more than willing to talk about their craft. An alternative is to have a speaker from the local college come in and speak about the history of film.

Have the students watch different films from different time periods and have them observe the differences in locations, props, and overall style. Involve the students in organizing a short film festival with the topic of "Film Through the Centuries."

ENGLISH LANGUAGE ARTS

Download or purchase a variety of scripts available to you. Just by skimming them, write down some of the structural elements that you see. The more the students read and study, the better screenwriters they will become. You may want to have a few screenwriting books on hand as well. Have the students think of some experiences they have had in school. Have them write a few scenes or even a whole short-film script dealing the topic.

Many films, notably foreign ones, are subtitled in translation. This is not only for language but also for the hearing impaired. Films from the U.S. are also subtitled in other languages. After watching scenes or an entire subtitled film, try to write subtitles in another language for some scenes of an American film or television show.

Film critics play a major role in Hollywood. Access and distribute examples of film reviews from magazines or local newspapers and have the students jot down what they think are some good ways to write about a film. What common thread or style do they see in the writing? Have the students then write a review of a movie they have recently seen. Encourage them to submit it to the school paper or even their local paper.

ARTS

Have the students look at some of the examples of storyboards and view a film to see the relationship between storyboards and what is onscreen. They could create a series of them for a film they have seen or one they would like to shoot.

Actors and actresses prepare a lot for their roles. Ask the students to list some of the qualities they think an actor/actress might need to possess in order to be believable. Have them watch an acting video or explore some of the books about the topic. They could conduct a series of mock auditions for roles or for their actual project.

As mentioned in the text, the director and director of photography must have a creative eye when it comes to seeing the whole scene in terms of a photograph. There are a wealth of good books and websites dedicated to photography and movie stills. Have students explore a variety of them in order to understand what photography-related skills they need to possess.

After a film is made, movie posters, stills, and artwork must all be completed to help promote the film. Have the students pick two newly released films and look up the "marketing" campaign for the film. After they study the elements for a bit (e.g., posters, trailers, advertisements, etc.), have them design and create a movie poster for a movie they have seen or will make.

Find out when there is a local film festival and encourage your students to attend. The possibilities might even exist for some volunteer work. Have the students become location scouts for a movie that will be in production. They can use preexisting scripts and a camera to log all the places they find.

TECHNOLOGY

Students could explore the more in-depth editing programs available to them. As with writing, the more time they spend at the controls, the more fluid, creative, and knowledgeable they will become. Students can explore the world of special effects in depth. Have them view a film or scenes and describe some of the cutting-edge special effects and ponder how they are created. They could then design their own special effects for a movie they or their peers are working on.

Some students may want to work with special effects and green screen technology, which you can use to superimpose anyone, anywhere, made possible with an iPhone and a green wall. With newer additions to technology like Adobe After Effects, where special effects can be added with a single click, students can create like never before. There are some great tutorials for both of these "added" extras if you want to dive in with your students.

PROBLEM-BASED LEARNING

PROPOSING A FILM PRODUCTION/ VIDEO EDITING SUITE IN A SCHOOL

Problem: The school does not have video editing facilities or adequate equipment for film/video production.

Solution: Have the students draft a plan that will be presented to the administration of the school by addressing the need for the above problem.

Students will need to research the ins and outs of designing a facility and filling it with equipment. They will also need to include a budget. They will need to consult handbooks, architectural plans, and other schools with such facilities. Also of importance is looking at any business that may supply equipment or grants for funds.

CONNECTING TO THE LOCAL COMMUNITY: A PUBLIC SERVICE ANNOUNCEMENT (PSA)

Problem: The area around your school has a high poverty rate or other social issue.

Solution: From preproduction to postproduction, students will design, script, shoot, and edit a public service announcement (PSA) that could be shown on a public access or news program. The theme of the piece should act as a persuasive mechanism to lead others to fight for the explained cause.

ORGANIZING A SCHOOL OR DISTRICT-WIDE STUDENT FILM FESTIVAL

Problem: Many schools in the surrounding region have great film/ video production classes and afterschool activities, but lack an outlet for presentation.

Solution: Have the students plan a film festival that will be held at their school or a local theater. This will involve the creation of entry applications and publicity contacts to distribute applications and to promote the event. A budget of the cost of renting a theater or facilities and possible awards and judgment should be made. Students could contact other festivals of the same nature in the surrounding region and find out what they will need to do to succeed.

FILMMAKERS AND FILMS OF NOTE

FILMMAKERS

Altman, Robert (1925–2006): *The Player, Nashville*

Burns, Ken (1953–): *Baseball, The Civil War*

Coen, Ethan (1957–) and Joel (1954–): *Fargo, No Country For Old Men*

Coppola, Frances Ford (1939–): *The Godfather* trilogy, *Apocalypse Now*

De Sica, Vittorio (1901–1974): *Bicycle Thieves, Umberto D.*

Edison, Thomas (1847–1931): inventor of the phonograph; Kinetoscope (with W. K. L. Dickson)

Fellini, Federico (1920–1993): *8 1/2, La Dolce Vita*

Ford, John (1894–1973): *The Searchers, Stagecoach*

Godard, Jean-Luc (1930–): *Breathless, Alphaville*

Hitchcock, Alfred (1899–1980); *Strangers on a Train, Psycho*

Jeunet, Jean-Pierre (1953–): *Delicatessen, Amélie*

Kubrick, Stanley (1928–1999): *The Shining, 2001: A Space Odyssey*

Kuleshov, Lev (1899–1970): "father of Russian cinema;" one of Soviet cinema's leading film directors and theorists; The Kuleshov Effect

Lucas, George (1944–): *Star Wars, Indiana Jones*

Luhrmann, Baz (1962–): *Moulin Rouge, Strictly Ballroom*

Lumière, Louis (1864–1948): *The Actualities*

Méliès, George (1861–1938): *A Trip to the Moon, Bluebeard*

Riefenstahl, Leni (1902–2003): *Triumph of the Will, The Blue Light*

Scorsese, Martin (1942–): *Taxi Driver, Goodfellas*

Spielberg, Steven (1946–): *Jaws, Schindler's List*

FILMS

400 Blows, The: Directed by Truffaut, 1959

A Trip to the Moon: Directed by Méliès, 1902

An Inconvenient Truth: Directed by Guggenheim, 2006

Apocalypse Now: Directed by Coppola, 1979

Arrival of a Train at La Ciotat, The: Directed by Lumière, 1896

Back to the Future: Directed by Zemeckis, 1985

Bicycle Thieves: Directed by De Sica, 1948

Caddyshack: Directed by Ramis, 1980

Citizen Kane: Directed by Welles, 1941

Close Encounters of the Third Kind: Directed by Spielberg, 1977

Delicatessen: Directed by Caro, Jeunet, 1991

Double Indemnity: Directed by Wilder, 1944

Duck Soup: Directed by McCarey, 1933

Hairspray: Directed by Waters, 1988

Horse Feathers: Directed by McLeod, 1932

Jaws: Directed by Spielberg, 1975

March of the Penguins: Directed by Jacquet, 2005

Mary Poppins: Directed by Stevenson, 1964

Moulin Rouge!: Directed by Luhrmann, 2001

Mystery Train: Directed by Jarmusch, 1989

Notorious: Directed by Hitchcock, 1946

O Brother Where Art Thou?: Directed by Coen, 2000

Oklahoma!: Directed by Zinnemann, 1955

Player, The: Directed by Altman, 1992

Psycho: Directed by Hitchcock, 1960

Rocky: Directed by Avildsen, 1976

Rope: Directed by Hitchcock, 1948

Searchers, The: Directed by Ford, 1956

Shadow of the Vampire: Directed by Merhige, 2000

Shining, The: Directed by Kubrick, 1980

Singin' in the Rain: Directed by Donen, Kelly, 1952

Star Wars: A New Hope: Directed by Lucas, 1977

Strangers on a Train: Directed by Hitchcock, 1951

Super 8: Directed by Abrams, 2011

Team America: World Police: Directed by Parker, 2004

Touch of Evil: Directed by Welles, 1958

Triumph of the Will: Directed by Riefenstahl, 1935

Vertigo: Directed by Hitchcock, 1958

STORYBOARD TEMPLATE

STORYBOARD TEMPLATE

PRODUCTION BREAKDOWN REPORT TEMPLATE

PRODUCTION BREAKDOWN
REPORT TEMPLATE

Prod. Date	Production Name	Director

Scene Numbers

I/E	Set	D/N	Pages

Description	Locations

Cast	Extras/ Atmosphere	Props

Makeup/Wardrobe	Equipment

Misc.	Notes

STUDENT INTEREST-A-LYZER

Name:_____ Date: _____

STUDENT INTEREST-A-LYZER

The purpose of this questionnaire is to help me become more familiar with some of your interests related to filmmaking. The questionnaire is not a test and there are no right or wrong answers, but at some point it may be necessary for you to do a little thinking to know what some of your interests might be.

As you read the questions, try not to think about the kinds of answers that your friends might write or how they might feel about your answers. Remember, no one will see your answers if you want to keep them confidential.

1. Imagine that your class has decided to create its own film production company. Each person has been asked to sign up for his or her first choice for one of the jobs listed below. Select your first and second choice.

   ___ Actor/Actress   ___ Scenery Design
   ___ Director   ___ Props/Location Scout (photography)
   ___ Musician   ___ Light/Sound
   ___ Business Director   ___ Marketing
   ___ Costume Manager   ___ Script Writer
   ___ Special Effects   ___ Camera Operator

2. Imagine that someday you will be the famous writer of a well-known film. What type of film will it be and what will the screenplay be about?

   Type of Film: _____

   The screenplay will be about: _____

   _____

   _____

   What would the title of your film be? _____

3. If you could be involved with a film of your choice, what type of film would it be?

   ___ documentary   ___ fantasy
   ___ science fiction   ___ mystery
   ___ musical   ___ adventure
   ___ classic   ___ horror
   ___ foreign   ___ drama
   ___ comedy   ___ animation

4. Please list five of your favorite films.

   1. _____
   2. _____
   3. _____
   4. _____
   5. _____

5. Have you ever been involved in a film class or as part of a group making a film?

   ❑ No   ❑ Yes (If yes, explain below.)

   _____

   _____

   _____

   _____

   _____

6. Imagine that a film is going to be made about your life. What would be the title?

   _____

   _____

7. Who would play you?

   _____

8. Why do you want to study filmmaking?

   _____

   _____

   _____

   _____

   _____

9. Do you have any questions or ideas you would like to share?

   _____

   _____

   _____

   _____

   _____

   _____

GLOSSARY

180-degree system: the editing of a film that ensures narrative continuity by dictating that the camera should only be placed on one side of an imaginary line, called the 180-degree line

B-roll: supplemental footage in a documentary that is intercut into the main footage (e.g., landscapes, buildings, etc.)

charcter cues: in a script, indications of which character is speaking a line of dialogue

character type: a certain type of character that can consistently be seen from film to film (e.g., cowboys in Westerns, detectives in film noir)

cinematography: a common term for all of the ways the camera captures the action

close-up: a camera shot that frames the subject filling nearly the entire screen; framing of the human figure from the neck up

computer generated imagery (CGI): special effects and graphics that are created on a computer in postproduction

continuity editing: a system of editing that maintains continuous and clear narrative action

coverage: filming multiple angles of the same scene

crit: short for critique; when students show their work to their peers to get feedback

cut (or straight cut): the joining of two shots together without space or overlap

cutaway: the interruption of an action by inserting a shot of something else

deep focus: using the camera lens and lighting to keep objects in both close and distant planes in focus

dialogue: the lines spoken by the characters on screen

dialogue overlap: in editing, carrying the sound of shot "A" over into the next shot

diegesis: the world of the film's story; everything the characters onscreen can see and hear is part of the diegesis

diegetic sound: any sound that has a source within the world of the film; sound the characters on screen can hear

dissolve: a transition between two shots during which the first shot is briefly superimposed over the second shot

documentary: a style of nonfiction filmmaking that presents real life events, people, and places

Dutch angle: a framing of a shot that is not level; also called a canted angle

editing: selecting and putting footage together

elliptical editing: shot transitions that leave out parts of an event

establishing shot: a shot, usually from a distance, that shows spatial relations among important objects in the frame

extreme close-up: a camera shot in which an object fills the frame, most commonly a small object or part of the body

extreme long shot: a camera shot in which the landscape or background dominates; the human figure is barely visible

fade: (1) **fade-in:** a black screen that gradually brightens as the shot appears; (2) **fade-out:** a shot that gradually disappears as the screen darkens

flashback: an editing technique that shows events that occurred earlier in the story

flash-forward: an editing technique that shows events that will occur in the future of the story

framing: using the edges of the frame to select what will be seen on screen

genre: the type or classification of films recognized by their familiar conventions

graphic match: two shots joined together to create a similarity of visual elements (e.g., color, shape, etc.)

high angle: a shot where the camera is placed above the subject, looking down

ingesting: in digital editing, the act of importing footage into a computer

Kinetoscope: an early device used to exhibit motion pictures to an individual

Kuleshov Effect: derived from Soviet filmmaker Lev Kuleshov's experiment where multiple cuts of various objects were intercut with identical shots of an actor's face. The resulting effect was a perceived change in the expression of the actor.

long shot: a camera shot that shows an object as small with the background dominating; framing the human figure from head to toe

long take: a shot that continues for an unusually lengthy time before transitioning to the next shot

low angle: a shot where the camera is placed below the subject, looking up

medium close-up: a camera shot which shows an object fairly large in the frame; framing the human figure from about the chest up

medium long shot: a camera shot which shows the majority of an object with the background still visible; framing the human figure from about the knees up

medium shot: a camera shot which shows an object in moderate size in the frame; framing the human figure from about the waist up

mise-en-scène: all the elements placed in front of the camera to be filmed; this includes the setting and props, lighting, costumes, makeup, and figure behavior

mobile framing: also referred to as camera movement; the change of framing during a shot

montage sequence: a segment of a film that summarizes or compresses an event into a shorter time than it might actually take

motif: an element in a film that is repeated for significance

movie trailer: a short montage intended to promote an upcoming movie release. The term "trailer" is used because trailers used to be shown after the feature in theaters

narrative: the story of a film

nondiegetic sound: sound, such as music or voice-over narration, that does not have a source in the story world

omniscient narrator: the disembodied voice that gives us information but doesn't belong to any of the characters in the film

pan shot: a camera movement on a stationary axis from right to left or left to right

parallel editing: also referred to as crosscutting, editing that alternates between two or more events occurring in different places

postproduction: the final phase of the production process that assembles the images and sounds into the finished film

preproduction: the first phase of the production process where the scripting and funding of the film occurs

presentation: one of the six shared genre conventions; the cinematic elements that distguish films

production: the process of shooting a film before the editing takes place

racking focus: the shifting of focus from one plane of the frame to another during a shot; also called pulling focus

score: instrumental music that is composed for a film

selective focus: setting up which parts of the frame will be in focus at any given time

setting: one of the six shared genre conventions; where and when the film takes place

soundtrack: prerecorded songs that help enhance the overall film

stars: one of the six shared genre conventions; the idea that audiences associate certain actors and directors with particular types of films

story formula: one of the six shared genre conventions; plot patterns and story structures that remain consistent throughout particular types of films

straight-on angle: the framing of a shot where there is no angle, just a natural straight ahead view of the subject

subgenres: a more specific way of defining and categorizing types of films

tableau: a still image that successfully uses mise-en-scène to define the genre

take: one uninterrupted run of the camera

themes: broad concepts that help define the meaning in film

tilt shot: a camera movement on a stationary axis that moves up and down

timeline: in nonlinear editing, the timeline is an interface that enables editors to lay a video project out in a linear fashion horizontally across a monitor

tracking shot: a type of camera movement that follows a subject's movement

two shot: a shot that depicts two objects balanced on either side of the frame

wipe: a transition between two shots during which a line crosses the screen, eliminating one shot and replacing it with the next

ABOUT THE AUTHORS

Jeff Danielian is the director of the La Salle Scholars Program in Providence, RI. He received his master's degree in educational psychology from the University of Connecticut and currently holds the position of Teacher Resource Specialist for The National Association for Gifted Children, where he is the editor-in-chief of *Teaching for High Potential*, coauthors the bimonthly column "Connecting for High Potential," and writes the monthly column "The Teacher's Corner."

Uriah Donnelly is a film professor, filmmaker, and musician based in Rhode Island. He received his master's degree in digital media from Rhode Island College. His courses include Introduction to Film, Introduction to Film Production, Preproduction: From Word to Image, and Film Production: Narrative Form. His documentary film, *Going Up Home*, is in regular rotation on PBS. This is his first book.

ABOUT THE ILLUSTRATOR

William Schaff is an artist and musician based in Warren, RI. A graduate of the Maryland Institute College of Art, Schaff has exhibited and lectured at numerous institutions, including the United States Air Force Academy, the Rhode Island School of Design, Amherst College, and East Carolina University. He is known for creating artwork for many bands, including Brown Bird, Okkervil River, Godspeed You! Black Emporer, Songs: Ohia, and The Mighty Mighty Bosstones.

For Product Safety Concerns and Information please contact our EU
representative GPSR@taylorandfrancis.com
Taylor & Francis Verlag GmbH, Kaufingerstraße 24, 80331 München, Germany

www.ingramcontent.com/pod-product-compliance
Ingram Content Group UK Ltd.
Pitfield, Milton Keynes, MK11 3LW, UK
UKHW030829080625
459435UK00017B/596